Legal Profession: Is It For You?

*A No-Nonsense Guide
to a Career in the Law*

Published in the
United Kingdom by Bruce & Holly

ISBN 978-1-54826-638-7

Also available as a Kindle ebook
ISBN 978-1-84396-473-5

Catalogue records for this book are
available from the British Library and the
American Library of Congress.

Pre-press production
eBook Versions
27 Old Gloucester Street
London WC1N 3AX
www.ebookversions.com

MISSION

To make the legal profession as accessible
to today's school leavers as it was to me when
I qualified more than forty years ago.

Legal Profession: Is It For You?

A No-Nonsense Guide to a Career in the Law

V. Charles Ward
(Solicitor)

BRUCE & HOLLY

Contents

INTRODUCTION

It is easy to think of the legal profession as being solicitors and barristers.

But as this book points out, there are at least five other ways to enter the legal profession. This includes the three support professions of paralegals, legal secretaries and barristers' clerks. What is good is that there is mobility within the legal profession. There are many solicitors working today who began their careers as legal secretaries, then using the knowledge and experience they collected along the way, qualified as Legal Executives before making that final leap into qualifying as solicitors. There are barristers who began life as solicitors and vice versa. All our judges are drawn from the ranks of barristers and solicitors as well as some legal executives.

For most solicitors working today, the route to qualification has been long, expensive and stressful, involving a three-year university degree followed by a year-long course of study for the Legal Practice Course. But an ability to pass examinations does not guarantee admission as a solicitor. There is a further hurdle which the would-be solicitor has to overcome.

To gain admission to the solicitors' profession it is necessary to complete a two year training contract with an organization providing legal services. But it is a competitive market where the demand for training places outstrips supply. It means that every year there are many would-be solicitors who have passed the Legal Practice Course but cannot gain entry to the profession because they cannot get training contracts. The position is similar for would-be barristers, who first need to complete a one year pupillage before their training is complete. If these were the only ways to enter the legal profession it would be unfair on thousands of would-be lawyers who have the abilities but not the financial resources or the time to undertake a three year university course or who miss out on getting a training contract or pupillage. Fortunately there are other ways to enter the legal profession which might suit someone of modest means who, perhaps, is trying to qualify whilst holding down a full time job or with pressing family commitments.

Roughly 25% of solicitors working today are former legal executives who have since passed the Legal Practice Course and converted their status from legal executive to solicitor. Many of those former legal executives would not have needed university degrees and can now be exempted from the need for a training contract to the extent that they can demonstrate that they already have the practical experience which a training contract would provide. A theme running through this book is that it is not just the law but the legal profession itself which is undergoing constant change. A welcome development is that the traditional distinctions between solicitors, barristers and legal executives have become blurred as these three branches of the profession move closer together.

Thirty years ago it was only barristers who could present cases in the High Court, the Crown Court, the Court of Appeal and the House of Lords (since re-named the Supreme Court). Now any solicitor who has obtained a Higher Advocacy Qualification can appear alongside barristers on equal terms. They can even wear wigs.

Becoming a Legal Executive is no longer the second tier profession it once was. Even the title has been elevated to 'Chartered Legal Executive'. Those with the required accreditation can also present cases in court and, like solicitor-judges, are now eligible for selection to the judiciary. Those Chartered Legal Executives who obtain 'Authorised Practitioner' status can also set up their own firms and compete head-to-head with other lawyers.

Barristers are no longer dependent on solicitors for their instructions. They can now take work from clients directly. For the savvy client this can mean a massive saving in the costs of running a case, as they are only paying one set of legal fees instead of two.

There are still limitations. The continuing restriction on barristers holding client money means that they cannot carry out transactional work for a client. Transactional work is still – for the time being - reserved for solicitors, chartered legal executives and licensed conveyancers. But how long will it be before that also changes?

This book is written for school leavers, university students and anyone else considering the legal profession as a career option. It may also be of interest to someone seeking a career-change in later life.

The book presents the legal profession as it exists today and how it is likely to change in the future. It explains how this ancient vocation can now be accessed by anyone with the right ability and commitment. It also provides the reader with a mass of historical information about the profession and how it has developed over the centuries.

Its early chapters challenge readers to consider their own reasons for wanting to enter the legal profession and whether that profession is right for them. It also takes the reader on a guided tour of that tiny part of London which has become the spiritual heart of the legal profession and explains its rich history. Later chapters explain the qualification process for each of the seven career options. But qualification alone does not make a successful lawyer.

It is why the final chapters focus on how a legal career can be progressed through specialization. It explains the legal market and the importance of choosing a specialization which is likely to be marketable both now and over the life of a legal career.

The author was admitted as a solicitor in 1976 and specializes in commercial and residential property. He began writing for publication in 1991 and between 1994 and 2000 wrote a regular weekly law page for Local Government Chronicle. He has also contributed frequently to Estates Gazette and Legal Executive Journal. He gained additional insight into the internal workings of the profession through his work as a Chief Conveyancing Examiner for the Institute of Legal Executives from 1996 to 2014, during which time he laid the foundations for a conveyancing syllabus which is still in use today. Much of the historical information in this book derives from the author's own personal recollection over a forty year career. Previous books by this author include Residential Leaseholders' Handbook, published 1996.

Chapter One

IS IT ABOUT THE MONEY?

Why do you want to be a lawyer? Is it about the money?

Yes. There is money to be made to be made in the law. On 27th October 2016 the London Evening Standard reported a record number of London lawyers earning more than £1m after a surge in lucrative takeover deals. An unprecedented 11 City firms exceeded the seven-figure average pay mark for partners in 2015, according to a survey carried out by The Lawyer Magazine. Again the best paid lawyers were at City based Slaughter and May, where equity partners were each taking home £1.9m.

On 1st June 2015 the Law Society Gazette reported that another big name, Linklaters, would be paying its trainees £42,000, rising to £68,500 for newly qualifieds and £98,500 for those qualified for three years. But not all lawyers are paid so handsomely.

Depending on who you ask, and according to the Daily Telegraph (23rd April 2015), average lawyer pay for a starter is £54,000 for the first five years, rising to £76,000 for someone qualified for 5-10 years; £100,000 for 10-15 years and up to £181,000 for someone qualified for more than 15 years. But not all lawyers would agree with those figures. One experienced criminal duty solicitor claimed that his average annual remuneration was more in the region of £25,000 to £35,000. And if the Daily Telegraph figures are the average, it must mean that half of lawyers are earning less than that average, perhaps substantially less. However much a lawyer earns depends on several factors, including the size of the firm within which they work and their particular specialism. With some specialisms being worth more than others it is about supply and demand. But the worst paid are Britain's 3000 sole practitioners.

There are solicitors who, for their own individual reasons, prefer to work alone instead of in partnership with other lawyers or as part of a larger organization. Annual earnings for sole practitioners can be a paltry £28,000. In fact if money is your object, you might be better off driving a London tube train.

Many years ago when I was researching a piece for Local Government Chronicle, I was astonished to learn that that the £29,000 annual starting rate for a first tier planning inspector was £2000 less than the basic salary for a tube train driver. Planning inspectors are Government appointees who have the power of life or death as regards land development. They are the people to whom you appeal when the local council turns down your planning application.

Fifteen years on and planning inspectors in London were

earning a more respectable £44,717 rising to £57,299 for Senior planning inspectors. Basic pay for tube train drivers had also risen in the same period and was then nudging £50,000 a year and with the highest paid driver reported as getting a cool £61,218 . Maybe it's all about clout.

As the first draft of this chapter was being written, there was a series of tube strikes over then Mayor Boris Johnson's plans to introduce all-night tube services at weekends. A year previously the strikes were about the proposed closure of ticket offices. Would a mass walk out by planning inspectors or legal aid lawyers grind London to a halt in quite the same way?

Even as this book is going to press, Southern rail drivers have rejected the offer of a £75,000 pay package to resolve a year-long rail dispute. So perhaps we are all in the wrong job.

Maybe driving down the same dark tunnels day after day in isolation doesn't appeal to you. Maybe you want a job which involves meeting people and where every day is a little different. Maybe you want a job which requires you to think creatively and help clients find solutions to problems. In many ways the law is a hand-holding service. Some people may come to you because they have a difficult problem and nowhere else to go. Others may want someone to safeguard their interests or guide them through a difficult transaction. What is constant about the legal profession is that it is always changing.

Four decades ago the signature sound of a solicitors' office was the 'clack, clack, clack' of the electric typewriter. Well that and the unanswered telephone ringing in the background. Today much of that bustle has gone. Typewriters are replaced by the silence of the computer keypad. In many organisations even the secretaries have gone. Back-to-back telephone calls have given way to email. Round table meetings are now conference calls. The sophistication of modern electronic case-management systems means that even paper files and documents could soon be consigned to history. But the changes are not just physical. Back in the seventies, the legal profession had restrictive practices which would make a trade unionist proud.

There was no competition. Other than a name-plate and gold lettering in the window, all other advertising was banned. Conveyancing fees were fixed according to a published scale. There were no contingency fees. Only solicitors could instruct barristers. Queens Counsel could not be instructed at all unless another junior barrister was instructed at the same time. Only barristers could appear in the High Court, Crown Court, Court of Appeal and House of Lords. Only solicitors could write letters on behalf of clients. All that began to change in the Thatcher years.

At the beginning of the 1980s the Law Society fought a series of losing battles against unqualified conveyancers who had set up business in competition with established solicitors. As they were not bound by any professional rules they could advertise and undercut in a way which qualified lawyers could not. It was only when it became obvious that these non-solicitor conveyancers were not going to be driven out of the market that the Government broke the monopoly by setting up a new profession with its own qualifications and regulatory standards. The tactic worked. Those who could meet the new regulatory standards became Licensed Conveyancers. Those who could not left the market. Order was restored. Around the same time other reforms were gathering pace.

In the mid-1980s the first solicitor advertisements appeared. But their design and content was restricted. Only 'tombstone' newspaper advertisements were allowed: which in practice were little more than a name-plate stating the name of the firm, its contact details and the categories of work carried out. Solicitors were not able to claim any specific expertise or quality which might indicate that they were any better than anybody else. These restrictions were progressively eased to the advertising free-for-all which exists today.

In 1990 the best performing solicitor-advocates, whose talents were previously restricted to the magistrates and county courts, were given the opportunity to apply for a higher advocacy qualification which would enable them to appear alongside barristers in the higher courts. But there was a catch.

Solicitor-advocates were still not allowed to wear wigs: which meant that they were too often mistaken for the court usher. Equality was restored on 2nd January 2008 when, for the first time, solicitor-advocates were permitted to wear wigs.

In 2004 the solicitors monopoly on instructing barristers was broken with new Direct Access arrangements, which would enable members of the public to instruct barristers directly. These were initially restricted at first to selected categories of work and progressively expanded to cover all areas of the law. However even under a direct access arrangements, barristers can do no more than provide advice and representation for their clients in courts and tribunals. Whilst barristers can now write letters for their direct access clients, they cannot issue legal proceedings or undertake transactional work. Another revolution has been in the language of the law.

Like steam trains, well-worn, centuries-old words like 'plaintiff' and 'subpoena' were consigned to history overnight as part of the 1999 Woolf reforms of civil procedure: replaced instead by bland and more politically correct substitutes like 'claimant' and 'witness summons'. Though telling someone that you are going to issue a witness summons does not carry the same emotional punch as the threat of a subpoena. Though it is strange that more than half a century after the death penalty was abolished, the phrase 'Warrant of Execution' is still used to describe the seizure of goods by a county court bailiff. Language changes continue with the re-naming of the Lands Tribunal into the clumsier "Upper Tribunal (Lands Chamber)" and the Americanisation of the House of Lords into the Supreme Court. Sadly the recent abolition of juries in libel trials by the 2013 Defamation Act means that we may no longer see the likes of the late George Carman QC.

Gorgeous George, as the press dubbed him, was amongst that rare breed of specialist lawyer who did not only act for celebrities but, through his work and his successes and his style, also became a celebrity in his own right. Carman's gift was his ability to engage emotionally with jurors. He made his name in the 1979 Jeremy Thorpe murder trial, when he achieved Thorpe's acquittal. His technique was demonstrated in his closing words to jurors in that case:

"Thorpe had won millions of votes from the people of this country but now come the twelve most precious votes of all."

Then pointing at each individual juror in turn he said,

"yours", "yours", "yours" ...

He also secured an acquittal for comedian Ken Dodd in his 1989 trial on tax evasion charges, when he said to the jury, "Some accountants are comedians. But comedians are never accountants."

But Carman was most famous for his work in the libel courts. Amongst his most notable successes was his demolition of East Enders actress Gillian Taylforth in her 1994 libel action against The Sun newspaper. Taylforth had sued after the newspaper had claimed that she had been seen by a policeman given oral sex to her boyfriend Geoff Knight in their Range Rover in a slip road off the A1 in Hertfordshire. Taylforth denied it. She said that she had only undone Knight's trousers to relieve the pain of his pancreatitis and that she had massaged his stomach.

Days before the jury were to delivery its verdict, Carmen sprang new evidence in the form of five year old video footage of Taylforth at a party simulating oral sex with a large German sausage. There was nothing more to be said.

Celebrity divorce lawyer Fiona Shackelton came again to public attention in the McCartney divorce case when she faced a determined litigant-in-person in the form of Heather Mills. But Shackleton's victory did not come without cost when the angry Mills threw a jug of water over her head. Shackleton had previously won fame in a succession of Royal divorces in which she acted for Prince Andrew and later for Prince Charles in the most high profile divorce of all.

Anyone pulled up on a speeding charge and facing the loss of their licence and livelihood might want to engage Nick Freeman, motoring lawyer to the stars. Freeman's celebrity clients have included Sir Alex Fergusson and David Beckham. Freeman quickly earned the name 'Mr Loophole' for his ability to tease out the tiniest technical flaws in seemingly the most straightforward of road traffic prosecutions and secure acquittal.

What all celebrity lawyers have in common is that each has carved out a unique niche for themselves in a 200,000 strong legal profession. Later in this book we will see how specialization is the key to any successful legal career. But there is something else shared by all successful lawyers which we will look at later in more detail: Passion. Celebrity is not guaranteed.

The nearest Britain has had to a celebrity judge - at least in living memory - was the late Lord Denning. He was the country's chief civil judge (known as Master of the Rolls) from 1962 until he retired in 1982 aged 83. Known as 'The Peoples Judge' Denning spoke with a Hampshire brogue which might have won him an audition for a place in Pirates of the Caribbean. He also courted controversy in his passion for putting justice before the technical requirements of the law. And unlike many of today's senior judges you didn't have to be a lawyer to understand his judgments. Some of them read like a story book. Take the opening words of his dissenting judgment in the 1977 case of Miller v Jackson, in which he waxes lyrical. It concerned a neighbour's complaint of nuisance from cricket balls coming onto their property.

> *"In summertime village cricket is the delight of everyone. Nearly every village has its own cricket field where young men play and the old men watch."*

But the biggest change is in relation to the numbers of practising lawyers. According to a 23rd March 2010 Daily Mail report, the number of practising solicitors expanded from around 32,000 solicitors in the early 1970s to 115,00 at the date of that report. The current tally is more than 132,000. Assuming the same rate of growth, there will be more than half a million solicitors by 2060. And three million solicitors 100 years from now. In the same period the number of barristers has ballooned six-fold from around 2,500 in the 1970s to nearly 16,000 today.

In fact it would seem that every week new solicitors firms are springing up on every high street frontage, often within yards of each other. With more than one lawyer for each 400 of population it is now easier to see a lawyer than to see a doctor. What is most surprising is that in spite of that expansion, there is still enough work to go round. Has there ever been a lawyer who will admit to being anything less than rushed off their feet? Another change is in the way solicitors are trained. In the 1970s it was a free for all. But also affordable. In those days there were no student loans, only grants.

Two A levels in any subject was enough to get anyone enrolled on the Law Society's Part I course at The College of Law, at Lancaster Gate or Guildford. Then followed a year-long introductory course on English Law, taking in constitutional law, civil and contract law, crime and land law. It was a cram course. The volume of information to be absorbed meant that it had to be dictated and memorised. Understanding would come later.

The big shake out was the end of year examination. Only half of candidates passed. You knew if you had passed because, on the morning the results came out, The Times, which was then a broadsheet, published a list of successful candidates. If you name was on the list, you had passed. If not, you had failed. Getting a Training Contract, or Articles of Clerkship as it was then called, was also easy.

As articled clerks were barely paid more than £10 per week, they were cheap labour. But it didn't matter. They were there to learn a trade. Almost every firm had its articled clerks, including the one man bands. In fact it was sometimes the smallest firms which offered the best experience, because the articled clerk was at the heart of everything which was going on. What killed off the market for training contracts was the Law Society's insistence on minimum terms and conditions for trainee solicitors. Think about the maths.

If you are a sole practitioner struggling to take home £30,000 a year, why would you want to spend £16,000 of your hard earned money employing a trainee? And then have to spend time training them as well? So it means that the only firms now taking on trainees are a minority of larger firms which are willing to make that investment.

Chapter Two

A WALK IN THE GARDEN

That tiny part of London bounded to the South by the River Thames; to the north by High Holborn; to the east by Blackfriars Bridge and to the West by Aldwych; is the spiritual home of the legal industry. If you become a lawyer you will get to know it well. Its history begins with King Henry III's strange announcement on 2nd December 1234 that,

"Nobody providing legal education should be located in the City of London."

As there was no-one prepared to argue with the great King, the fledgling legal profession began to establish itself on lands immediately to the West of the City. Within a century, the dissolution of the Knights Templar enabled the legal profession to establish itself on land formerly owned by the Knights. A symbol of that mystical past is the Temple Church, which sits in the midst of the barristers' chambers at the Inner and Middle Temples. It dates back to 1185 and is modelled on the Church of the Holy Sepulchre in Jerusalem. Look inside and see the chiseled image of one of those brave warriors above his tomb.

Starting at Blackfriars Bridge walk westwards along the Victoria Embankment past the Unilever Building and what used to be City of London School. Keep walking and cross John Carpenter Street, Carmelite Street and Temple Avenue. Those roads were once the home of the newspaper industry before it moved to Wapping. Keep walking and on your right you will see the gardens of the Inner and Middle Temples. A few yards on from those gardens you will come to Temple Underground Station, which is on the District and Circle Lines. Take some refreshment at the station café and buy a copy of Private Eye from the news stand opposite. Across the road you will see Arundle Street, which would take you straight up to The Strand. But instead we are turning left along Temple Place.

First on the right is Surrey Street, which is where we are we are going. Walk northwards towards Aldwych. Half way up on your left you will see the sign directing you to the Roman Baths. Take a left along the covered alleyway known as Surrey Steps and follow it round until you come to a glass window, through which you can see the old Bath. It's smaller than you would imagine. More the size of a jacuzzi – and dry of course. Then re-trace your steps back to Surrey Street and keep walking up. A couple of yards further and on your left you will see the defunct Aldwych Underground Station. It marks the end of the former branch line from Aldwych to Holborn, which could have held the title as the world's shortest railway. It closed in 1994 and is now only used for filming.

Turn left at the top of Surrey Street, where it meets The

Strand, and walk a few yards. On your left you you will see the palatial Somerset House. It was built in 1776 and extended in 1831 and again in 1856. Somerset House was the main administrative building for the Family Court until its move to First Avenue House, 42-49 High Holborn. It housed the Principal Probate Registry as well as the Divorce Registry.

When registration of births, marriages and deaths was introduced in 1837 and for the next 150 years, Somerset House was the place where all family records were kept. Before internet sites such as Ancestry UK made family research accessible and affordable to all, Somerset House was where you would go to research your family history. But it was a painstaking, longwinded and uncertain process beyond all but the most dedicated family historian. Opposite Somerset House on the corner of Aldwych is India House. Next to India House (looking Westwards) is the impressive bank-like building known as Bush House .

Until Stamp Duty was abolished by the Finance Act 2003 in favour of the newly introduced Stamp Duty Land Tax, The South West Wing of Bush House housed the main Stamp Duty office for London and the south east. It was a walk-in service which had barely changed since Stamp Duty was first invented in 1624 as a tax on documents. Above the front door-way you can still see the words 'Inland Revenue'.

After a completion of a property transaction, conveyancers would complete a one page 'Particulars Delivered' form and then take it with the conveyance, transfer or lease to the Bush House Stamp Office, which was through the left hand doorway on the ground floor of the building. The PD form itself required basic details about the transaction: such as the property address, how much was paid for the property, and the names of the solicitors' firms who handled the sale and purchase.

Once inside the building the lawyer (or more commonly the articled clerk) lined up at the PD counter and handed the original title deed and the completed PD form to a bored official sitting behind the counter. The bored official would take a moment to study and compare the title deed with the PD form. Then if everything was right, the official would signify approval by stamping the title deed with a square red rubber stamp to certify that the required particulars had in fact been delivered. But if there was any imperfection in the way the form was completed, or if it was felt that a plan of the property was required, both PD form and title deed would be angrily thrown back. But even if you got the coveted red stamp, your job might not yet be done.

If the value of the property exceeded a stated threshold there would also be stamp duty to be paid. This meant going to another counter with your PD'd document and stamp duty cheque, which would be passed through a post-office type glass screen to another official, who would take it away to a stamping machine.

Several thuds later, the official would return to the counter and hand the document back with a series of posh red stamps impressed across the front to evidence the amount of duty paid on it. Funnily enough the officials working the stamp duty machines never seemed as bored as the man with the rubber stamp. Perhaps it was a fun job.. Stamp duty machines have now gone. The one-page PD form has been replaced by a multi-page Stamp Duty Land Tax Form requiring as much detail as a self-assessment tax form and which is submitted on-line.

Now walk east-wards back along the North side of The Strand until you come to a large gothic building. It looks like a medieval cathedral. But it's not a cathedral and it's not medieval. It is the Royal Courts of Justice and it was opened by Queen Victoria in 1882. If you've got the patience to go through the modern airport-style security and explain your purpose, you will reach the cavernous marble interior. Inside, the monastic theme continues with long narrow passages and stone stairways leading to its 88 court rooms. The Royal Courts of Justice is Britain's largest civil courthouse and houses the Court of Appeal as well as the High Court. Within the court complex, more recent buildings have been added including the West Green Building, the Queen Elizabeth Building and the Thomas More Building. When you have finished looking round it, step back outside and turn left and walk a few yards to the junction with Chancery Lane.

The Lane gets its name from its association with the High Court of Chancery, which existed there from the twelfth century. As you walk upwards along Chancery Lane, the first major building you will pass is The Law Society at 113 Chancery Lane with its metal arch above the entrance steps. The Society itself was founded 2nd June 1825 under the name of The Society of Attorneys, Solicitors, Proctors and others not being Barristers' and did not become 'The Law Society' until 1903. It moved to its current building in 1832 and was the regulatory body for the Solicitors Profession until that function was taken over by the Solicitors Regulation Authority in 2007. However the Society remains the body representing solicitors.

If you visit the Law Society be sure to go upstairs to the Library on the first floor. It contains books dating back centuries, the oldest of which are accessed from narrow metal landings and spiral staircases. It is also the library of last resort, containing legal records inaccessible elsewhere.

One example is the Finchley Enclosure Act 1811, which was needed to prove ownership of a piece of land for which no known title records existed. But it was known that the land had once been an isolation hospital and during the War years a decontamination centre. By chance it was discovered that the land was shown as a highway gravel pit on an 1815 Finchley Enclosure Award. But a copy of the Act itself was needed to complete the jigsaw. Attempts to Google the Act had proved fruitless: as were visits to the National Archive at Kew and the London Archive at Farringdon. But the Law Society Librarian found it within five minutes. And it was in mint condition. And there was another discovery.

Shaded in blue on the 1815 Enclosure Award is a large area of land set aside for proposed reservoir. The Regents Canal Company had bought the land in 1811 but sold it on again in 1818 before Finchley was flooded.

Around the corner from Chancery Lane is Lincolns Inn Fields where the modern land registration was born in 1862. 32 Lincolns Inn Fields remained the Land Registry HQ until 2011, when its operation moved to Croydon and its existing premises were sold to the London School of Economics for £37.7 million.

Immediately past the Law Society Building and on the same side of the road is the small Barristers' outfitters, Ede and Ravenscroft, with its wooden green frontage. The company was established 1689 and is where you might go to buy a judge's wig, a barrister's gown, a detachable wing collar or the preaching bands which are worn with it. Walk a little further and on the left there is a large wooden double-gated Tudor entrance. It is the Gatehouse of Lincoln's Inn, the oldest of the four Inns of Court and was constructed in 1564. Walk further to the top of Chancery Lane to the junction with High Holborn. Cross to the other side of High Holborn. Next to the Cittie of York Public House is the narrow passageway opening out into Grays Inn.

Sadly what has disappeared from Chancery Lane are the legal bookshops. The latest to go is Hammicks, which was situated at the bottom of Chancery Lane at the junction with Fleet Street. It closed its doors on February 2015 to become an Itsu fast food outlet. Another legal publisher, Sweet and Maxwell, had a long frontage on the same side of Chancery Lane as the Law Society Building. Both retailers still exist but for the time being only as ghosts in the ether, although Hammicks has stated its intention to re-open in another location.

Books can still be bought on-line but you can no longer browse or window-shop. At the time of writing, Wildy & Son, another law book seller, still has its small shop within Lincoln's Inn Archway, which is off Carey Street behind the Royal Courts of Justice. The shop has been there since 1830 and, in terms of physical appearance, has barely changed. It has a second shop at 16 Fleet Street.

What make Wildy's different from the other mainstream law retailers is its low key presence. It's one of those oldy worldy shops you might stumble across in a market town and wonder how it still survives. The other thing that makes it different is its trade in second hand books: invaluable for a struggling student. A lesser known former incumbent of Chancery Lane was the Law Notes Lending Library: a small bookshop which existed half-way along the eastern side of the street. It rented out text books to Law Students at about half the cost the student would otherwise have to pay to buy the books new. On their return they would be rented out to the next set of students. But the shelf life of a law book is short.

Because the law is always changing, a law book begins to date after around three years. But this is not a problem for on-line publications, which can continually update with each new legal development. So why would you want to rent a second hand book?

Law Notes Lending Library closed its doors in the Nineties and without trace. There was also a monthly Law Notes Magazine issued free by the College of Law to its students for more than 140 years: during which time it had barely changed. It had been in the form of a shiny white pamphlet and contained updates on changes in the law and recent cases. Each issue also included a four page playlet in the form of a conversation between a fictitious 'Mr Worldly Solicitor', his junior partner 'Nephew Tom' and 'Ariadne', their Articled Clerk. Shortly before its demise and in an attempt to modernize, the traditional white colour changed to blue.

If you want to know what a walk through Victorian London might have looked like, felt like or even smelt like, go through one of the passageways leading from The Strand into the Inner and Middle Temples. Then walk downhill towards the exit at The Victoria Embankment. Do it after dark when the gas-lights burn. Wait till the rush hour has gone and the only sound is your footsteps on the cobbles.

Chapter Three

BARRISTERS

Barristers are the gladiators of the legal profession. They are their clients' hired champions. But they fight with words not with sword or sticks. It is also the oldest branch of the legal profession, dating back to the days of the Knights Templar. Although a barrister's chambers can be situated anywhere, every barrister has to be a member of one of the four Inns of Court.

Barristers earn their living within an adversarial system of law which still exists in the UK. Adversarial means that each of the opposing parties independently presents their cases and their evidence to a neutral umpire, which in civil cases is the trial judge. In criminal cases that umpire is the magistrates or the jury. Rules of engagement also allow each party test the strength of the opponent's case through cross examination.

During the course of a trial the judge is a listening bystander, interjecting only to maintain the flow of the proceedings or to adjudicate on issues of procedure or fairness. At the conclusion of the trial, after the last question has been asked and the final speech has been made, the judge, magistrate or jury has to choose between the two cases, based only on the evidence they have seen and heard. In civil cases that choice is made on the 'balance of probabilities', which means that the credibility of the two cases are hypothetically weighed against each other, and judgment given in favour of the case which is considered most likely. In criminal cases a conviction requires proof beyond reasonable doubt, which means that the accused cannot be convicted if there is any realistic prospect that a mistake might have been made. If a civil claim is found proved or a criminal case results in a conviction the judge will, after hearing more barrister speeches, decide what damages should be awarded or penalty imposed.

Outside the courtroom, and with Hannibal-like cunning, each barrister will have prepared their battle plan, anticipating the points or questions which the opposing counsel is likely to make or ask and devising strategies to neutralise them. Inside the courtroom, advocates refer to each other as 'my friend' or 'my learned friend'. Even boxers have friends. But there is no room for friendship inside the ring. Respect for an opponent - yes. Courtesy - yes. But don't expect favours. Because no quarter will be given. Advocacy is the loneliest job. Because all responsibility rests on your shoulders.

For a client, choosing a barrister is like picking a horse. Everyone wants to back the winner. In many cases barristers are appointed on the personal recommendation of someone who has used them and was pleased with the outcome. Otherwise it is about studying form. All barristers publish profiles about themselves, listing significant cases in which they have been involved and more particularly those they have won. A good advocate cannot guarantee to win a bad case. But a bad advocate can easily lose a good one. But a barrister's work goes beyond preparing for trial and standing up in court. Just as important is what a barrister can do to prevent a case coming to trial by facilitating a negotiated settlement. There is good reason for this. Litigation itself is a poker game. Think about it.

You put some money on the table. Your opponent matches it and raises the stakes. You put more money in the pot. So does your opponent. And the process is repeated - and repeated. But as the case approaches trial, the cost of staying in the game escalates to the point that both parties have put so much money on the table that neither can afford to back out. To make matters worse it is also a double-or-nothing game. The cost of backing out is that you will also have to cover your opponent's costs and perhaps sell your house to do so. No wonder more than 90% of contested cases settle before reaching trial. But the impossible cases to settle are the neighbour disputes, where the parties hate each other so much that they cannot even speak.

In 2012 John Edwards and Mary Kendrick had to pay out tens of thousands of pounds to cover the costs of neighbours Stephen and Barbara Evans after they wrongly took down the Evans' new fence, which they said was sited in the wrong place, when it did mark the correct boundary. But the prize goes to Belgravia residents Hameed and Imran Faidi whom in 2009 incurred a £140,000 legal bill after pursuing to the Court of Appeal their complaint that they were disturbed by the sound of high heels tap tap tapping on the £100,000 oak floor of the upstairs flat. The Court of Appeal ruled that there was no requirement on the upstairs owner to cover the floor with carpet. Lord Justice Jackson then made the following comment about the costs of the case,

> *"If the parties were driven by concern for the well-being of lawyers they could have given half that sum to the Solicitors Benevolent Association and then resolved the dispute for a modest fraction of the monies left over."*

Finally it is worth mentioning that not all barristers are actively involved in court work. There are also several thousand non-practising barristers who have the qualification but not a practising certificate entitling them to appear in court. Some are employed by the Crown Prosecution Service whilst others work alongside other lawyers in solicitors' firms.

Chapter Four

SOLICITORS

The word 'solicitor', with its sexual undertones, is a strange way to describe someone whose job primarily involves the marshalling of documents: whether those documents be of the traditional paper variety or increasingly the virtual documents which appear when you log onto a computer screen and disappear into the ether the moment you log off. Those documents could be anything from leases, wills, land-transfers, letters or emails through to the written statements in a murder case. In fact it could be said that the key difference between the vocation of a barrister and that of a solicitor, is that barristers are speakers and solicitors are writers. There is another difference.

Within the professional hierarchy, solicitors are traditionally the first point of contact for anyone requiring legal assistance or representation. In fact until the introduction of direct access arrangements, it was only solicitors who could issue any instructions to barristers. With more than 150,000 participants it is also the largest constituency in the legal profession.

Could it be that our earliest professional forbears earned their title by hanging around court doorways like time-share touts soliciting business for the barristers within? A modern equivalent of those medieval brethren might be the no-win-no-fee claims-consultants who frequent our town centres urging passers-by to fill out accident questionnaires with the promise of riches to come. But it was not long before those early solicitors began undertaking legal work in their own right. So the profession was born.

The American word 'attorney' more accurately describes a solicitor's role. It means 'legal representative'. Though like many Americanisms, it started out as an English word. The first solicitors were also known as 'attorneys', until the word fell out of use during the 19th Century. But it has not disappeared entirely. For the time being there is still an 'Attorney General', who is the Government's Chief Legal Adviser and has other State functions, including the review of over lenient sentences. The phrase Power of Attorney still exists to describe a situation where a person delegates to someone else the right to represent them and deal with matters on their behalf. It is sometimes used when someone is going abroad for a long period and would like someone else to look after matters in their absence. That 'someone else' is their Attorney. The use of the word Attorney to describe the work of a solicitor is something which could return to the UK since the Law Society relaxed its rules on the naming of firms. Until 1997 the name of a solicitors' firm had to include the name of a current or former partner. Now it can call itself anything within reason. So it is perhaps only a matter of time before we see US style Attorneys at Law re-opening on our high streets.

Another big difference between solicitors and barristers is that the solicitors' profession is desk-based whereas barristers are a travelling profession. In fact you can often spot a barrister on their way to court. They are the men and women with the pin-stripe suits lugging the over-large box-shaped attaché cases jammed with papers and reference materials. The big give-away is still the sheaf of papers tied together with the traditional pink, green or white ribbon. Though again times-are-a-changin' as the court system goes on-line and it cannot be long before pink ribbons and wheeled attachés are completely superseded by the lap-top. It is also worth mentioning that there are also many solicitors who carve out successful careers as solicitor-advocates. But again there are key differences between solicitor and barrister advocacy.

Whereas a barrister can practice in any court anywhere in England and Wales, most solicitor-advocates tend to practice in those magistrates and county courts which are local to them. In fact if you watch cases in your local magistrates' courts you may notice that although each client and case is different, it is often the same solicitor-advocates appearing before the same magistrates and the same justices-clerks. You may even notice the rapport that has built up between the magistrates, the clerks and those solicitors. It is that dynamic which can make those solicitor-advocates so effective.

They know the mind of the judge or magistrate who is sitting in front of them. They know what will create empathy and what will antagonize. They have already made their mistakes and have learned from them. They will know what is coming and will be prepared for it. Their client will be similarly briefed.

But the bread-and-butter for many solicitors' firms has always been conveyancing and probate. There were some firms which never did anything else. Everyone moves house. Everyone dies. But conveyancing is no longer the cash-cow it once was. It is prone to the booms and busts of the housing market. It has also become too competitive. If you are a typical high street firm offering a traditional high street service, how do you compete with a conveyancing factory offering an on-line service at £175 plus VAT? Another staple is matrimonial work.

According to figures published by the Office for National Statistics, a marriage has a 42% chance of ending in divorce. In 2012, the year William and Kate tied the knot, so did 262,000 other couples. So if 42% of those marriages break down, that will mean 110,040 couples heading for the divorce courts. Each divorce will require two sets of divorce lawyers to deal with the fall-out from the broken relationship. That may include arrangements for looking after children, splitting the assets and dealing with any long term maintenance arrangements. But there are also newer areas of work for lawyers to get involved. One of these is employment law.

Until 1970, getting sacked or downgraded in your employment was just something which happened. There was nothing you could do about it. Yes – if it happened after 1965 you might qualify for a small redundancy payment. But that was the extent of your rights.

Then came the politically controversial Industrial Relations Act 1971: which was a first attempt to regulate industrial action which, up to then, had been immune from civil suit. The Act had been introduced by the Heath Conservative Government, which had won power in 1970. A year earlier in 1969, Barbara Castle, Labour's Secetary of State for Employment and Productivity, had published a Government White Paper, *In Place of Strife*, which first mooted the idea of regulating industrial action. But against division within the Wilson Cabinet and trade union opposition, the idea was quietly dropped.

The newly formed Industrial Relations Court (IRC) failed its first test the following year when, against the backdrop of a national miners' strike, it was called upon to deal with unlawful secondary picketing by dockers of the Chobham Farm Container Depot. On the Company's application, the IRC first issued an injunction banning the unlawful picketing. The Court's ruling was ignored. The Court then issued an order committing the ring leaders to prison for contempt of court. Five dockers were arrested and imprisoned at Pentonville, in a case which became known as 'The Pentonville Five." But they were released within a week.

Against a campaign of work-stoppages, marches and the threat of a general strike, it was the Official Solicitor who diffused the situation by taking it upon himself to apply to the Court of Appeal for the dockers' immediate release on the grounds that the IRC had no powers to order imprisonment and because the Company's own evidence was not as watertight as it should have been. After that the IRC never again sought to imprison anyone and after Harold Wilson snatched power back in the 1974 general election, the IRC was abolished, to be replaced by new industrial tribunals. But one legacy of the 1971 Industrial Relations Act lives on.

A by-product of the 1971 Act was the new concept of Unfair Dismissal as a ground for statutory compensation. It was to balance the withdrawal of the unrestricted right to take industrial action. It was that right not to be unfairly dismissed which was adopted by the incoming Labour Government, although no-one could have then foreseen the industry which unfair dismissal claims would later become. At first the compensatory entitlements for unfair dismissal were minuscule and, as recently as 1999, were capped at £12,000.

Under legislation introduced in the early days of the Blair Government, that limit jumped to £50,000 and currently stands at £76,574. But there is one type of unfair dismissal where the prospect of compensation is unlimited: where race, sex or any other unlawful discrimination can be proved.

Is was as a result of a case brought to the European Course of Justice by a Miss Marshall, that it was declared in 1994 that there could be no statutory cap on compensation where unlawful discrimination was involved. Ms Marshall had previously won her claim for sex discrimination against an attempt by her NHS employer to make her retire because she had passed the statutory retirement age for women, which was then five years earlier than for men. She had successfully argued that her employer's behaviour was discriminatory. But at that

35

time compensation was capped at £6,000. It was that statutory cap which Ms Marshall successfully challenged. Immigration law presents another opportunity for solicitors looking for new areas of work: against the backdrop of the current middle east crisis and the resulting population displacements.

Chapter Five

CHARTERED LEGAL EXECUTIVES AND LICENSED CONVEYENCERS

At just over 20,000 strong, Chartered Legal Executives are a smaller profession than solicitors or barristers. Their work mirrors that of solicitors and can be just as specialist but until 2015 there were limitations on their abilities to set up businesses offering services directly the public. That changed as a result of the Legal Services Act 2007. There is now a process by which Chartered Legal Executives can seek authorization to set up their own businesses offering conveyancing, probate, litigation, advocacy and immigration services directly to the public. The only difference between that and solicitors is that their right to offer services directly is not automatic.

They are represented by the Chartered Institute of Legal

Executives (CILEX), which is based at Kempston, near Bedford. Before obtaining Charter Status in 2012 the organization was known as the Institute of Legal Executives. The Law Society first sponsored its establishment in 1963 as a means of giving formal professional status to what were previously known as Managing Clerks.

These were solicitors' clerks who had become legally proficient to the extent that they could deal with their own case-loads and manage less experienced colleagues. In 1892 they had formed their own organization, The Managing Clerks Association. In 1963 those managing clerks were given the new title of Legal Executive and the opportunity to obtain accreditation through a new system of training and examination.

But whilst numbers of solicitors and barristers are booming, the numbers of students training to be legal executives remains stubbornly small. Is it because it has not fully thrown off its managing clerk image and is still seen as a profession which assists instead of carrying out work in its own right? That is no longer the reality.

Even before the 2015 regulatory changes, the profession had evolved to the extent that legal executives could represent clients in court, become judges and become partners in solicitors' firms, including such blue chip names as Wedlake Bell; Field Fisher Waterhouse and Freeth Cartwright. So why aren't there more trainee legal executives?

Perhaps it comes down to marketing. The Chartered Institute has a quality product. But what's the point of having an excellent product if no-one knows about it? Could it be that like other academic institutions in the UK, the Chartered Institute is uncomfortable selling itself in the market place? It is something to which Britain's universities have already had to come to terms.

With almost every municipal technical college having re-branded itself a university, and with annual tuition fees of up to £9,000, it is small wonder that prospective students want to shop around. Higher education has become a buyers' market. It is the same with professional institutions. Why would you train to become a Chartered Legal Executive, when you can train to become a solicitor or a barrister? That is the challenge which the Institute faces.

But there is one big selling point which the Chartered Institute has over the other two: it is arguably the only branch of the legal profession (other than Licensed Conveyancers) which is accessible to someone with a full time job; full time family commitments and who simply cannot afford to take three years out to obtain a university degree before they can even start their legal training. And there is something else.

Becoming a Chartered Legal Executive is not a one stop shop. It can also provide a stepping stone to qualification as a solicitor. In fact until recently the only way in which someone could qualify as a solicitor without a university degree was by qualifying first as a Chartered Legal Executive. To give an example, many successful lawyers are former legal secretaries who made use of their office experience first to train as a legal executive, before taking the final step towards becoming a solicitor. Without CILEX they would not have been able to do it.

Licensed Conveyancers are the newest branch of the legal profession. They owe their existence to the conveyancing wars of the early 1980s when the Law Society unsuccessfully tried to prosecute out of existence the rash of unqualified conveyancers who had sprung up to challenge the monopoly which solicitors then had over conveyancing work. The Law Society's position was not helped by the argument that it was trying to defend an indefensible monopoly situation in which consumers were being held to ransom.

It was against that stalemate that the Government legislated to break the solicitors' monopoly by allowing anyone to set up as a conveyancer provided they were sufficiently qualified to do the job and could meet regulatory standards. It did so by setting up an entirely new profession with its own routes to qualification and regulatory framework. It was the Administration of Justice Act 1985 which set up this new profession. Licensed conveyancers are now entitled to set up business alongside solicitors firms and compete with them. However the only legal services which they are able to offer directly to the public are conveyancing and probate services. Like CILEX, the licensed conveyancer route provides affordable access to the legal profession for someone who is already holding down a full-time job or other family commitments.

Chapter Six

THE SUPPORT
PROFESSIONS

In these days of political correctness it seems that no-one is a clerk any more. The former Town Clerks of our towns and cities have become Chief Executives. Articled Clerks have become trainee solicitors. Solicitors' clerks have become paralegals. But in spite of the advance of new-speak, there still remain some bastions of clerk-ship. For the time being Justices' Clerks are still called Justices Clerks. And Barristers' Clerks are still called Barristers' Clerks. Although the job of a Barristers' Clerk is largely administrative, it is an essential part of the legal profession and with its own particular skill-sets.

Behind every celebrity there is a manager. In the case of Elvis Presley it was Colonel Tom Parker. It was always Parker who promoted Presley, got him the bookings and negotiated his fees. As Presley himself once said about Parker, *"I don't think I'd have ever been very big if it wasn't for him. He's a very smart man."*

For 'celebrity' read 'barrister'. For 'manager' read 'barrister's clerk'. The relationship is the same. The barrister makes the appearances and wins the cases. The barrister's clerk makes the bookings and negotiates the fees. Walk into any barristers' chambers and look for the Clerks' Room. It's usually one of the ground floor rooms nearest the building entrance. It looks like a dealing room: which essentially it is. It is the noisiest room in the building.

Look inside and you will see half a dozen men and women sitting behind computer screens. Some will be engaged in telephone conversations, usually with firms of solicitors. They will be discussing a barrister's availability for a particular case. They may also be negotiating that barrister's fees for the case. Others may be dealing with correspondence or planning their barrister's day. There will also be a stream of barristers coming in and out to check on their appointments or to find out whether a particular document or email has arrived for them. Clerks are also people of influence.

They are the first point of contact for anyone enquiring about a barrister's services. Often a solicitor will approach a particular chambers without knowing quite which individual barrister they want to instruct. They will however know that this particular chambers specialise in the particular area of law with their client is involved. If it is a property dispute, they might go to Falcon Chambers. If it is to do with employment, it might be 7 Bedford Row. Or to Doughty Street Chambers for human rights. But how do they choose which barrister is right for the case? In short they will rely on what the Clerk tells them.

The Clerk might first of all tell you what barristers they have available for a particular case. It is likely that the most experienced barristers already have a full case list, so it may be a case of slotting in. Having found out which names are available, the Clerk is then in a position to quote a range of barrister expertise and prices in the same way that Kwik Fit might sell you a tyre. Once the solicitor has chosen a barrister with the right skills and experience for the job, the haggling will begin. The solicitor will try to get the best deal for the client. The Clerk will try to get the best price for the barrister. Why? Because many barristers' clerks are paid on commission.

The starting salary for a junior clerk may be as little as £15,000 rising to £25,000. For senior clerks the range is from £30,000 to £80,000. But there are some barristers clerks who can earn more than a QC.

On 19th October 2000 The Independent ran a report on the highest paid barristers' clerks. Top of the pile was David Grief, Senior Clerk of Essex Court Chambers whom, according to a survey by The Lawyer Magazine, earned £350,000 in a single year. But he was not alone. The runners up earned £320,000 and £280,000 respectively.

Although they are not lawyers, barristers clerks need to know enough about court procedures to plan their barristers' schedules and understand the needs of the solicitor instructing them. In many cases the clerk may know more about those day-to-day procedures than that solicitor. Clerks also need to be emotionally engaged with the ups and downs of barrister life.

When the barrister wins, it will be the clerk who joins in celebration with lawyer and client. When the barrister suffers an unexpected defeat, it may be the clerk who provides the shoulder to cry on. But like everything else in the law, the situation is changing.

With the rise of direct access, many barristers are now choosing to work solo and advertise their services direct to the public. Their house or flat becomes their 'Chambers'. Telephone them and they will answer in person. Ask them about their fees and they will tell you straight. There is no middleman. But for most barristers, having a clerk offers convenience. It means they can focus on their cases instead of haggling about fees or getting involved in the time-consuming administrative paraphernalia of the law. Barristers Clerks are represented by the Institute of Barristers Clerks, 1 Garden Court, Temple EC4Y 9BJ.

With the progressive replacement of electric typewriters by word processors from the beginning of the 1980s, it had been predicted that up to 75% of secretaries would be made redundant. It never happened. Instead there was an explosion in the volume of paperwork. But what has affected the market for secretaries are the new ways of working with which many lawyers now have to conform.

With the support of modern technology, many organizations now expect their lawyers to be more self-sufficient in the physical production of their work. Shorthand petered out in the 1970s, having been eclipsed by audio. Now the dictating machine has all but gone. Voice recognition systems, as an alternative to manually transcribing a minicassette, have never really come up to expectations. You will have interacted with voice recognition systems whenever you telephone a call centre and, instead of using a touch tone, you are prompted to state in a few words the reason for your call. How often does the voice recognition system get it right?

The beauty of dictation, whether given face-to-face to a stenographer or spoken into a dictaphone, is that it enables documentation and correspondence to be produced quickly and in volume. Take that facility away and the whole process slows down. Even if you can touch-type, you can't type as fast as you can speak. Traditionally the measure of a good secretary was not only how accurately she typed but also at what speed, as expressed in words per minute or 'WPM'.

An average secretary might manage a comfortable 60 WPM. Top secretaries might double this to 120 WPM, effectively doing the work of two colleagues. Such secretaries were valued because producing work quicker meant greater profits for the firm. What is strange in many modern organizations is that the people who have retained their secretaries are the people who least need them. They are the CEOs and other senior management who spend most of their time in meetings or promoting the business instead of at the operational coal face of producing documents. What has made a difference to the way legal secretaries work is the advance of standardization.

All legal documents would have once have had to be typed up from scratch or by typing details onto a printed proforma, such as a standardised sale contract. If a serious mistake was made, and if it could not be discreetly corrected, the whole document might have to be typed all over again. In fact before word-processors, the same document might have to be typed up several times before the transaction could be completed. Take a standard residential lease.

There would be the initial draft lease prepared by the landlord's solicitors for the tenant. Once that was typed up and sent across to the tenant's solicitors, various hand written amendments would be made to the draft before the terms and format of the lease were finally agreed. Then the final agreed version would need to be typed up on thick paper for the client to sign. But of course as there were two clients - the landlord and the tenant - that final version had to be typed up twice: once for the landlord and the other for the tenant.

Proof reading the final version lease to pick up any hidden errors was a two person process: with one secretary reading aloud that typed up document, whilst the other secretary read the corresponding words on the 'travelling draft' with its many hand written amendments.

The availability of computer packages such as Practical Law means that, with a few clicks of a mouse, a standard 30-page residential lease will now self-generate in minutes and appear in front of you. It is then just about typing in the gaps, printing off and proof-reading for errors. Correspondence can be standardized in the same way. For the legal secretary it means that the job is now less about transcribing dictation at speed and more about being computer literate. It is about being able to take that messy cut-and-pasted document which a lawyer has given you and turning it quickly into something presentable for the client to sign. It is about being able to use the Land Registry Website to pull down title information about a property. Carrying out conveyancing searches has always been part of a legal secretary's job. Only now it's about making the search on-line instead of filling out a form and posting it off with a cheque. But there is one critical part of a legal secretary's job which has never changed and never will change.

It is often a legal secretary who will be the first point of contact for a prospective client who rings in enquiring about your firm taking on a piece of new work. It may be how the secretary handles that call which determines whether the caller hangs-up and looks elsewhere or asks your firm to act. Like a barristers' clerk, the secretary may even be asked to provide a recommendation as to which lawyer at the firm would be best placed to deal with the matter. Typical pay for a legal secretary might be £19,000. But for top flight city secretaries it could be as high as £38,000. They are represented by the Institute of Legal Secretaries and PAs.

At one time a paralegal would have been known as a 'solicitor's clerk'. Though as we have already seen, no-one is a clerk any more. A paralegal is a person with some knowledge and experience in the law and who is able to undertake legal work, but is not formally qualified as (or undertaking formal training to be) a barrister, solicitor, chartered legal executive or licensed conveyancer. In some organisations paralegals are termed 'legal assistants' and are within a formal career structure.

Many paralegals are law graduates who have not yet taken the route towards formal qualification. Some might not even be sure whether a career in the law is actually for them. Others may already be qualified lawyers but in other jurisdictions, most commonly: Australia; New Zealand; Canada; Ireland or South Africa. Many of those foreign lawyers, who are not tempted back to warmer climes, will go on to convert their qualifications to their English equivalent. Typical pay for a paralegal might be £19,000 rising to £27,000 for the most experienced. They are represented by the National Association of Licensed Paralegals.

Chapter Seven

JUDGES

No-one can go directly from college to becoming a judge. Every judge has to do have done something else first.

Traditionally judges were drawn from the ranks of barristers through a discreet appointments process and that remains the case for most judicial appointments. But as with everything else in the law, things are changing. In short the process is becoming more transparent. Becoming a judge is now a career option for solicitors. That career option has since been extended to Chartered Legal Executives but only to the level of District Judge.

Mention 'judge' and you might think of an elderly man in a wig glaring across a crowded courtroom. Yes there are judges like that. But not all judges are like that. There are many types of judge which, in order of seniority, could be listed as: Supreme Court Judges; Court of Appeal Judges; Circuit Judges; Recorders; and District Judges. The last, 'District Judges', is the new name given to people once known in the criminal courts as

'Stipendiary Magistrates' and in the county court as 'Registrars'.

All criminal cases start in the magistrates court and 95% of them finish there. But all magistrates courts owe their existence to the willingness of 23,500 men and women across society to give up hours of their time unpaid to try cases. Given their contribution it seems mean that political correctness now prevents those same volunteers from using the letters 'JP' or 'Justice of the Peace' to describe themselves on business and personal correspondence. Amongst those massed ranks there was always a handful of professionally qualified full time magistrates who received a salary or 'stipend'.

By contrast the core function of a County Court Registrar was always administrative in facilitating the smooth process of justice by ensuring that rules of litigation were correctly followed. Whilst their elevation to the title of 'District Judge' is belated recognition of the fact that they have always tried smaller cases themselves, the 'Case Management Function' still remains an important part of their work. But not all people carrying out judge-like functions have the name 'judge' in their title. As well as the courts themselves, there are many statutory tribunals, chaired by people who might be known as 'Member', 'Inspector' or simply 'Chairman'.

An example is the Upper Tribunal (Lands Chamber) which, until 2009, was known simply as the Lands Tribunal. It's function is to adjudicate on statutory land compensation claims, such as those arising from compulsory purchase of land by public authorities. It also the only body empowered by Section 84 of the Law of Property Act 1925 to modify or discharge obsolete contractual restrictions on the way land could be developed or used. Before the advent of modern town planning in 1947, the inclusion of such restrictions in title deeds was the only way an estate developer could retain long term control over the character and appearance of that estate.

The Upper Tribunal has a status equivalent to that of the High Court. Only the Court of Appeal and Supreme Court has higher status. Yet the person presiding over it has the humble title of 'Member'. The Upper Tribunal's junior cousins are First Tier Tribunals, who adjudicate in disputes between residential leaseholders and their ground-landlords on matters relating to service charges or the amount to be charged for a lease-extension. Like the Upper Tribunal, their judiciary are also known as 'Members'.

Becoming a judge might be the pinnacle of a career for barrister looking for something which is sufficiently well paid and offers job security. At the time of writing, pay for judges starts at around £107,000 for District Judges, rising to £134,000 for Circuit Judges and £180,000 for High Court Judges. But compare that with the £928,000 earned by Howard Godfrey QC as reported in the Daily Telegraph on 23rd March 2010.

Chapter Eight

WHERE
SOLICITORS WORK

It seems strange that whilst the number of solicitors in England and Wales increases year-by-year, the number of solicitors firms is falling. Yet this is a key statistic revealed in the Trends in the Solicitors' profession Annual Statistics Report 2014, which was published April 2015. It shows that in the year ending 31st July 2014 the total number of solicitors on the Roll increased 1,750 to 160,394 whilst during the same period the number of private practice firms registered in England and Wales fell 305 to 9,542. The statistics provide a mathematical snapshot of the profession as at 31st July 2014. But numbers themselves are meaningless without explanation. So let's look at the statistics in more detail.

Mention Roll of Solicitors and you might think of an ever expanding roll of parchment on which a wing-collared clerk inscribes the names of newly admitted solicitors, whilst crossing out the names of those who have died, retired or left the profession in less honorable circumstances. Using a quill pen of course.

Maybe it was once like that that. But it is now computerised. The Roll itself now exists only in legal fiction. Being 'struck off the roll' is still the term officially used to describe the permanent disbarring of solicitors whose behaviour has made them no longer fit to be called a solicitor. A surprising fifty or more solicitors meet this fate each year, sometimes because of deliberate dishonesty but more commonly because they are so disorganised that they put at risk their own clients' interests as well as the interests of everyone else who deals with them. Later we will look at the specific personal qualities which make a person into a lawyer: integrity being at the top of the list.

The term 'Master of the Rolls' is the official title of England's chief civil judge, who chairs the Court of Appeal (Civil Division) and is also in theoretical charge of this mythical 'Roll'. He has the last word as to whose name goes on it and whose name is taken off. The Lord Chief Justice is his criminal counterpart. Note the specific use of the word 'England' and not 'Britain' or 'United Kingdom'. Scotland and Northern Ireland have always had their own separate systems of justice. For the time being Wales operates under the same legal system as England, so reference to 'England' also include Wales.

Although at the last count there were 160,394 solicitors on the Roll, only 130,382 of those lawyers could be said to be 'practising'. To qualify as 'practising', a solicitor must hold a Practising Certificate. These are issued annually each November by the Solicitors' Regulation Authority, which is the body with statutory responsibility for regulating the Solicitors Profession. A practising certificate is required before a solicitor can offer arms-length legal services to a client. A current practising certificate is also required before a solicitor can exercise their right to represent clients in court. In some respects applying for a practising certificate can be likened to taxing a car. There is the annual fee to tax the car. But it is not just about paying the fee. Before the Driver and Vehicle Licensing Agency will accept payment, it will require confirmation that the vehicle is insured and has a current MOT certificate. It is the same with a solicitors' practising certificate.

Before the SRA will issue a practising certificate it will require confirmation that the solicitor has the required professional indemnity insurance and has kept themselves up to date with new professional developments. And there is also fee of several hundred pounds for issuing the practising certificate plus as contribution towards the Compensation Fund for those solicitors working in private practice.

The Compensation Fund is a mutual fund set up to compensate anyone who has suffered loss as a result of dishonest conduct on the part of a solicitor. In 2014 the Fund paid out £23M So what about the 30,000 solicitors who are on the Roll but do not hold a current practising certificate? There may be several reasons for this.

Some will be retired solicitors who are no longer offering legal services but who want to retain their professional status. It will include women on maternity or child care leave who are taking a temporary break from the profession. It will also include qualified solicitors whose job does not involve them offering legal services directly to the public but for whom a legal qualification may be an essential requirement. A law lecturer provides the obvious example.

Around 75% of the profession work in private practice. This means that they work for privately owned firms offering legal services directly to the public or to companies on an arm's length basis. But such firms exist in all shapes and sizes. In 2017 CMS UK, Olswang and Nabarros merged to create a super-firm with more than 4,500 lawyers spread across 65 offices in 36 countries. Of those, around 2,500 lawyers are based in the UK, with more than 1,000 at partner level. Against that, around one quarter of law firms are sole practitioners. Some work from small high street offices, others work from home. Others have joined 'virtual firms,' where they trade under the firm's banner but for all practical purposes work as self-employed consultants. They are represented by the Sole Practitioners Group, which also acts as a lobby group. There is also variety in the type of work which private law firms do.

Most high street firms offer a range of main-stream legal services to the general public. At one time their existence was evidenced only by the gold lettering in their windows. But most high street firms now display a sign listing the particular legal services which they offer. These will commonly include: conveyancing; probate; divorce; accident claims; neighbour disputes; landlord and tenant and crime. But not all firms will offer everything. As well as solicitors, most medium to large high street firms will also include a full complement of Chartered

Legal Executives, paralegals and legal secretaries. Some firms may have only a single office and one solicitor. Others may have twenty solicitors spread over several branch offices.

The largest solicitor firms operate out of city centres and their clients are big companies, equity funds, public sector organisations or utilities. Their work is more likely to involve very high value transactions or litigation. Examples include: estate development; company formation; mergers and acquisitions; town centre leasing. Many of these firms also have an international presence, such as Kennedys, which has offices as far afield as Hong Kong and Dubai. These commercial firms are also more likely to specialise both in terms of the work they do and in their clientel. For example Berwin Leighton Paisner's big client is Tesco. Trowers and Hamlin is the blue-chip firm for housing associations. Capsticks began in the 1980s as a tiny niche firm (see below) defending Regional and District Health Authorities against medical negligence claims. It is now a large firm offering a wider selection of services. But its core client is still the NHS. What the largest commercial firms offer corporate clients is not only expertise across a range of professional disciplines (from company mergers and acquisitions to house-building) but also the ability to pull in massive resources at short notice to deal with a major project which has to be completed within deadline.

Niche firms are tiny firms specializing in a particular area of the law to the virtual exclusion of everything else. For example if you are involved in a trade-mark dispute, you would not go to a high street conveyancing firm. You would want to go to someone who specializes in trade mark disputes. Yes – you could go to one of the big city firms who offer specialism in everything. But you would be paying city rates. An alternative may be to go one of the smaller niche firms who can offer you the same expertise but at lower cost and perhaps with a more personal service. As we have seen, Capsticks began as a tiny niche firm offering medical-defence to the NHS before expanding to the National firm it is today but without shedding the core characteristics which made it what it is. A smaller example of a niche firm is Sophie Khan & Co, which specializes in claims against the police.

Virtual Firms are the new kids on the block. They are real firms with a real head office, real solicitors, real clients and real back-up facilities. But they owe their existence to the internet. And there is another key difference: the solicitors are not bound to an office desk. They work remotely: usually from home. They are not employed directly by the firm but on a consultancy basis. Each has their own client-following but access to the firm's accounting and other back-office facilities. They do not earn a salary. Instead the fees they earn from their clients are split between the firm and the self-employed solicitor-consultant. In that respect they operate more like a barristers' chambers. As a centralized hub. It provides an alternative for those lawyers who prefer to work solo but wish to avoid the overheads of a stand-alone office. An example of a virtual firms is brand-leader Setfords. Another 18% of solicitors work 'in-house' for a company or a public-sector organization.

Although most companies send out their legal work to

external solicitors firms, many larger companies employ some lawyers directly to act as 'Corporate Counsel'. They are the people to whom Company Directors will contact for advice. They also act as gate-keepers, providing the link between the company and its external lawyers and may in some instances make the referrals. But is not enough just to know the law. The skill of corporate counsel is a thorough understanding of the company's internal workings and the market within which that market operates. The exception is Scottish and Southern Energy (SSE) which, at the last count, maintained a team of 63 lawyers under the banner, 'SSE Legal Services' whose work involves electricity substation leases and associated wayleaves. Around 15% lawyers are employed by companies.

Councils are another big employer of lawyers. However unlike private companies, most local authorities will try to do as much legal work as they can in-house and maintain a sufficient complement of legal staff for that purpose. Look inside the back pages of the Law Society Gazette and you will always find a raft of quarter-page advertisements for local authority lawyers across several professional disciplines, most commonly: town planning; housing; child-care; adult social services; property and general litigation. However as a local authority lawyer progresses up the ranks the work tends to become less operational and more administrative.

Many local authority chief executives are practising lawyers: an example is solicitor Charlie Adan, who was appointed Chief Executive of the Royal Borough of Kingston Upon Thames in April 2016. She previously worked as joint chief executive with

Babergh and Mid-Sussex District Councils. But only a tiny proportion of their day involves actual legal work. The latest trend is for local government legal departments to combine together to form Shared Services Organisations. These are intended to operate like private solicitors firms, charging out their work according to a fixed hourly rate and offering economies of scale and a wider range of expertise. An example of a shared services organization is HB Public Law, which is based at Harrow and serves the Councils of Barnet; Harrow; Hounslow; Aylesbury Vale and Buckinghamshire. Around 4,000 lawyers are employed by local councils.

The GLS (or Government Legal Service) is the umbrella term for around 2000 lawyers working across a range of Government Departments, from the Home Office through to the Department of Environment, Food and Rural Affairs. Technically their only client is The Government. Accordingly their job includes advising Government Ministers and also translating ministerial announcements into workable proposals, including drafting out the regulations and orders which will implement them. They also oversee the procurement of goods and services for Departments and appeals in courts and tribunals across the country to defend official decisions. They handled an estimated 66,000 cases during 2015-2016. Much of the work of a Government lawyer is politically sensitive, complex and in the public eye. Another 2,500 lawyers work for the Crown Prosecution Service presenting cases in magistrates courts.

Any school, college or university offering training to would-be lawyers, requires a team of law-lecturers. Those lecturers do not have to be practising solicitors or barristers but need the same level of legal knowledge as if they were practising lawyers. And they also need to know how to teach. Training the next generation of lawyers can be a career choice. Or it can provide additional and rewarding income for a practising lawyer with time on their hands.

Go to your doctors' surgery over the Christmas or holiday periods and, as likely as not, you will be seen by a locum. They are providing temporary cover whilst your doctor is away. They may have the same professional qualifications as your regular doctor but they will know nothing about you or your symptoms other than what is on the screen in front of them. There are many locums who spend much of their professional careers providing temporary cover whilst regular doctors are away. It is the same with the law.

Someone has to be engaged to provide temporary cover whilst the regular lawyer is away on holiday, or sick, or is on maternity leave. In many organisations (particularly local government), locum lawyers make up a significant proportion of their workforce and are engaged to deal with higher than expected levels of work (which can be most of the rime). The essence of locum work is 'easy-in and easy-out'. It is easy to hire a locum. It is easy to fire them. Most locum contracts can be terminated on a week's notice either side. Whilst some locums are employed directly, most work through agencies. The client-organisation pays the agency according to the number of hours worked. Then the agency pays the locum. The amount the client organization pays the agency is always higher than the amount paid by the agency to the locum. The difference covers the agency's overheads plus an element of profit.

There are many reasons why a lawyer may choose to work locum instead of seeking permanent employment. The pay can be substantially higher, particularly in the public sector. It also offers flexibility both for employer and client. It particularly suits lawyers approaching the end of their career who do not want a permanent full-time work commitment with a single employer but the ability to take time away when they need it.

Chapter Nine

HOW LAWYERS CHARGE

There is a significant difference between what lawyers earn and what they charge out to their clients. We saw in the first chapter that average pay for lawyers at the beginning of their professional careers is £54,000: equating to just over £25 per hour. Yet those same lawyers may charge their clients more than £150 per hour. Why the difference?

The answer is that what the lawyer charges the client has to cover more than their own salary. It also has to cover their share of office overheads and a reasonable profit for the firm. As a rule of thumb a typical firm might expect each of its lawyers to generate an income equating to three times their annual salary: one third to cover their own salary; another third to cover office overheads and the final third as profit for the firm. These will be set as annual targets for each lawyer. Those lawyers who can meet or exceed their targets will progress within the firm. Those who consistently fall behind will eventually be asked to leave as it will no longer be profitable for the firm to retain their services. Typical hourly charge out rates for a high street firm might be:

- Partner or director - £280
- Junior lawyer - £140
- Paralegal/trainee - £90

In setting its hourly rates, a firm will first have aggregated together its wage bill and other office overheads plus a reasonable profit element for the owners of the firm. That aggregated figure is then divided between the number of hours in a working year to calculate the minimum hourly rates which the firm has to earn for each working hour just to break even. One of the problems with hourly rates is that it rewards inefficiency. Applied strictly it would mean that it is always the slowest and most inefficient lawyer who gets paid the most. No client is going to stand for that. It is why most clients want to know exactly how much they will be asked to pay for a piece of work.

For routine household conveyancing transactions it is relatively easy for a solicitors firm to offer fixed quotes. If they are completing many such transactions each week, they will know how many hours on average it will take one of their conveyancers to complete a transaction of that type. In short, the quotation is a pre-estimate of the time the transaction is expected to take to complete. If it takes longer, it is the solicitors firm which will bear the loss. If it is completed quicker, the firm's profit will be that little bit greater. Many conveyancing quotations will be qualified by the words, 'assuming that there are no unforeseen complications' – or words to that effect. It means that the firm can revise its quotation if a problem occurs during the course of the transaction which will require significant additional work to resolve. But the client would first have to agree the revised price. Quotations will usually increase according to the value of the property being bought or sold.

It seems that every minute there are radio adverts opening with the words, 'Have you been injured in an accident which was not your fault?' The advertisement will then go on to offer you 'free' legal services on the basis that the firm's fees will be paid by the party which caused the accident. Only their services are not really free – any more than an estate agency's services are free up to the point they sell your house. What it means is that the firm takes the risk of the litigation. If they don't win your case, they won't be paid – but they will have still have had to bear their own salary and office overheads in their unsuccessful attempts to pursue your accident claim. But if they win they won't just want to be paid their hourly rate. They will want something extra in return for having taken on the risks of your case. It is called a 'success fee'. If it can be recovered from an opponent's insurance company, all well and good. But if not?

Most other legal work is carried out at the lawyer's quoted hourly rate. Their terms and conditions will be set out in a Client Care Letter which lawyers are required to send out to their clients at the outset of any new piece of work. The letter may provide an estimate as to what the work is likely to cost as well as details of the person who is going to carry out the work and the person to whom you can complain if you are not happy with the service provided. But that estimate is never guaranteed. If a client is not happy with the fees which have been charged it can be challenged using the firm's own complaints procedure followed by the referral to the Legal Services Ombudsman if the client is determined to pursue matters that far.

Chapter Ten

THE WORK LAWYERS DO

Later we will see how specialization can be the key to a successful legal career. The age of the generalist is long gone. Every lawyer must find a specialization on which they can build their professional reputation. But for now we will provide an overview of the main types of work within which lawyers make their careers. Here they are.

Conveyancer

Conveyancing remains the staple for many high street firms. Until recently many firms never did anything else. But the sheer competitiveness of the conveyancing market has meant that many of those firms are having to work to smaller margins and look for more profitable areas of work in which to diversify. Conveyancing work can be divided and sub-divided between many narrow specialist areas. However the main distinction is between Domestic Conveyancing and Commercial

Conveyancing.

Domestic Conveyancing is what most high street firms do. It is about mainly acting for private clients in the purchase and sale of houses and flats. Some of those clients will be moving home. Others may be buying to let. Like most areas of the law it is a high pressure job. Clients and estate agents just won't leave you alone. They will be on the phone to you daily to find out when contracts are going to be exchanged and when the transaction is going to complete. Estate agents have a special interest because they are paid on commission. The quicker the transaction exchanges and completes, the quicker they get paid.

Since the 1980s traditional domestic buy-sell conveyancing has diversified out into new specialist areas including: statutory lease extensions; freehold enfranchisement (where leaseholders club together to buy out their freehold); shared ownership and right-to-buy (where a local authority tenant buys their home at a discount).

Commercial Conveyancing generally involves the purchase and sale of business premises for commercial clients. Whilst most of the big commercial transactions are carried out by the big city firms for big clients, some commercial transactions are carried by high street firms for their small business clients. Although the law and technical processes are the same for both domestic and commercial conveyancing, each requires a different skill set. Domestic conveyancing predominantly involves the transfer of a house or flat from one person to someone else.

The job of the sellers' and buyers' conveyancers are to work together to ensure that the interests both parties are sufficiently protected and the transaction proceeds to a smooth exchange of contracts and completion. Another party involved in most domestic sales and purchases is a mortgage lender. Again it is the buyer's lawyer's responsibility to ensure that the lender's position is fully secured. As domestic conveyancing is so standardized, it is all about following procedures and being alert to any warning signs when anything is not quite right.

By contrast most commercial transactions are all about negotiation: just as much between solicitors as between clients. And whereas new residential leases follow a standardized format which is acceptable to mortgage lenders, each commercial lease is a tailored document which is likely to contain complex provisions as to how the property is to be maintained, insured, used or altered. Each one is a negotiated document. Any commercial lease for a period longer than five years is likely to contain provisions entitling the landlord to increase the rent at five-yearly intervals. There are well-drawn commercial leases. There are badly drawn leases. It is the job of the commercial conveyancer to know which is which. Getting it wrong will be expensive.

There are some types of conveyancing which cross the boundaries between commercial and residential conveyancing. An example is estate development (see below) where a law firm acts for a housebuilder in the acquisition of a potential development site and then again on the sale of the completed dwellings to individual plot purchasers. Since the Leasehold Reform, Housing and Urban Development Act 1993, statutory residential lease-extensions and the statutory buying-out (by leaseholders) of their ground-landlord's freehold interest have become a specialist area for residential conveyancers and is one which is likely to grow in the future as leases shorten. It is also a specialist area which crosses over with property-litigation (see below).

Taxation of property transactions has become more of an issue for conveyancers, with complex rules about Value Added Tax, which apply to some property transactions but not others, and at different rates. A more recent headache is the introduction of the 3% Stamp Duty Land Tax surcharge on second homes. And that is on top of SDLT rates of up to 12% even when the surcharge does not apply. The issue for any residential conveyancer costing out a prospective transaction is: does the surcharge apply? Or does it not apply? The answer is not always clear-cut.

Residential Landlord and Tenant

Until 15th January 1989, standard legal advice to anyone thinking of letting a residential property was 'don't'. Under the 1977 Rent Act, once a tenant was allowed into a property, they could be there for life. And on their death, their tenancy could transfer to another family member who was living with them. And even when there were grounds to evict a defaulting tenant, actually getting possession was, for the landlord, a slow and expensive process. And even where a tenant was in default, recovering possession could not be guaranteed. Whether the defaulting tenant stayed or went was entirely at the discretion of the judge. To make matters worse, even after a rent had been agreed, a tenant could later apply to a rent tribunal to get it reduced. No wonder the private rental market dried up. But now it seems that everybody is a buy-to-let landlord.

It was Margaret Thatcher's 1988 Housing Act which revitalized the private rented market by introducing the modern assured shorthold tenancy which enables a landlord to end it and regain possession on giving just two months notice. Assured shortholds survived the Blaire/Brown Labour Governments of 1997-2010 and remains today the most common way of letting residential property. And a whole industry has grown up around it, with new products such as buy-to-let mortgages and buy-to-let developments, by companies such as Galliard. Whilst in theory shortholds can be ended quickly, the landlord still needs to go to court to evict tenants who refuse to go. But provided the correct procedures have been followed, recovery of possession will eventually be granted, no matter how long-winded the process.

So standardized have shorthold tenancies become that most are dealt with by letting agents without involvement by lawyers. But it is the moment something goes wrong that a lawyer will have to pick up the reigns. Typically that will arise when tenants fail to pay their rent or otherwise default or do not move out after the tenancy has ended. Whilst shortholds were originally intended to provide a simple risk-free way to invest in the residential lettings market, in recent years it has become overlaid with an increasing number of regulatory traps relating to: the independent safe keeping of tenant-deposits; the need to carry out formal identification checks on incoming tenants; the safety of furniture, gas and electricity; and the amount of information which has to be given to in incoming tenant. Get it wrong and the landlord may end up with a tenant from which they can neither collect rent nor evict. More work for the residential lettings lawyer.

Property Litigation

This mainly covers disputes between landlords and tenants – both residential and commercial. The other potential for property litigation is disputes between neighbours as regards the alignment of boundaries, the exercise of rights of way or other rights associated with property, or nuisance-behaviour. But it is commercial leasing which makes property-litigation into a specialist area of the law with some very high sums at stake. Commercial lettings are less regulated than residential lettings and with fewer statutory protections for leaseholders. Anyone taking on a commercial property is bound by the terms of their lease. No matter how unfair or one-sided those terms may appear to be, judges won't interfere with them. If the lease says that the rent will increase by 20% each year – when price-inflation is only 3% - then that 20% is unfortunately what the tenant will have to pay. No wonder that the bulk of property-litigation work involves the interpretation of commercial leases. Other than the Landlord and Tenant Act 1954, which provides a statutory right of renewal for some business leases, the only statutory framework for commercial leases is that which applies to property generally. Unlike residential lettings, landlords don't always need a court order to repossess at the end of a commercial lease or if it has become forfeit following breach of the tenancy terms. Landlords can sometimes just change the locks. But doing so without the correct legal advice can be financially dangerous for a landlord.

The other specialist area for property-litigators relates to residential leasehold service charges. Whilst commercial landlords only have to look at the terms of their leases, residential ground-landlords have to circumvent a maze of regulation and procedures governing recovery of residential leasehold service charges. Note here that we are talking about 'ground landlords' who own the freeholds of blocks of flats – not buy-to-let landlords. The annual ground-rent payable by a leaseholder to their ground landlord might be a miserly £10 a year. But those ground-landlords still have the legal responsibility of maintaining, insuring and managing those blocks of flats and then trying to claw back their expenditure via annual leasehold service charges. Get the process wrong and that expenditure may be irrecoverable. Residential property litigation also involves First Tier Tribunal Work (previously known as Leasehold Valuation Tribunals). When it comes to residential leasing, the work of the First Tier Tribunal involves: adjudicating service charge disputes; assessing the price payable to a ground-landlord for a lease-extension or on the exercise by leaseholders of their statutory right to collectively buy-out their ground-landlord's freehold; and other statutory issues, such as right-to-manage. Specialist property litigators can also be divided between those who predominantly act for landlords and those who act for leaseholders.

Probate

Everybody dies. Everybody who dies leaving significant property or financial assets or valuable items will need somebody to collect together their estate and distribute it according to their Will or the rules of intestacy. Whilst the client is still alive, the work of the probate lawyer covers;

◆ Drawing up wills;
◆ Advising on inheritance tax planning and helping to put in place schemes to minimize future inheritance tax liabilities for an estate.

And after someone has died;

◆ Applying for Probate or Letters of Administration if there is no will;
◆ Collecting in an estate and distributing it according to the testator's wishes – or according to the Rules of Intestacy if there is no will;
◆ Dealing with any claims against the estate or disputes or other issues between beneficiaries, including claims under the Inheritance (Provision for Family and Dependents) Act 1975, by close family members who feel that they have been unfairly

cut-out or short-changed under a will.

Winding up an estate will also involve at least one conveyancing transaction, where the deceased owned a property which needs to be sold or transferred to beneficiaries. It can also quickly become litigious where there are disputes between family members or involving other third parties, which are preventing completion of the process.

Matrimonial

The number of divorces is falling. But that is only because more couples are choosing to live together instead getting married. But with some 40% of marriages breaking down, there will always be work for divorce lawyers. Whenever a marriage breaks up there will be assets to be split and (where children are involved) satisfactory arrangements put in place for their future welfare. Getting the divorce is easy. The difficult part is resolving the ancillary issues, such as:

+ How are the assets to be split between the parties?
+ Who gets to look after the children and what rights will the absent party have to see them and take them out?
+ How much should be paid by the absent (or richer) party to the other to maintain that other party and any children living with them?

In all these issues it is the interests of the children which the courts will consider paramount. Much more important in fact than which party was to blame for the divorce. Adultory may provide the innocent party with grounds for the divorce but it doesn't give the innocent party any advantage when it comes to splitting the finance. 'Resolution' is an organization with a 6,500 membership of family lawyers and associated professionals to promote non-confrontational resolution of matrimonial disputes.

Employment

There are employment lawyers who act for claimants. And there are employment lawyers who act for employers. As we have already seen, employment law as we know it had its roots in the ill fated 1971 Industrial Relations Act. There are now an estimated 80,000 unfair dismissal claims each year by aggrieved ex-employees against their former employers with average payouts of around £12,500 where no discrimination is proved. But the jackpots are reserved for those ex-employees who can successfully establish some form of discrimination, with average payouts of around £20,000 and a top payout of £470,865. At one time it was just race, sex or disability discrimination. But the list has since grown and additional categories include discrimination on grounds of: sexual orientation; age; religion or belief; marital status, and transgender. In fact it would seem that there now a discrimination claim for everyone. A surprising statistic is that at £23,000, the average payout for sex-discrimination beats race-discrimination by more than £3,000. But the work of an employment lawyer is not just about fighting or defending employment claims. Just as important is the work they do to advise employers on ways to prevent claims arising in the first place. And it is not just ex-employees who can claim. There are also compensation payouts for anyone who can show that they have been unfairly refused employment.

A less contentious aspect of an employment lawyers work concerns the Transfer of Undertaking (Protection of Employment) Regulations, which kick in whenever ownership of a business is being transferred – or even where services are just being outsourced to a different supplier. TUPE (as the regulations are known) will then ensure continuity of employment for existing employees in relation to the work which is being transferred. In that situation, the existing staff will transfer across automatically to the new business-owner or contractor and on the same employment terms and conditions as they had before. But there are exceptions, the new employer may have its own plans for reorganising the way the work is carried out, and TUPE gives them the flexibility do this. But there are sensitive processes to get right - on which an employment lawyer is best placed to advise. The issue of pension entitlements for transferring employees – as well as dealing with pension-deficits - is a particularly complex area for employment lawyers

Crime

With more than six million crimes committed each year in the UK, there will always be work for lawyers willing to give up their time to attend police stations at any time of the day or night. It is not the highest paid work because most of it is legally aided. Whilst a motoring conviction rarely involves loss of liberty, loss of a driving licence may still have other far-reaching consequences as regards a person's work or career. Many lawyers have however carved out successful and interesting careers, defending accused individuals in the magistrates and Crown courts.

Such work requires an expert knowledge of police and criminal investigation procedures as well as of the criminal justice system generally. As well as attending trials, the work of a criminal lawyer also include making bail applications and making pleas in mitigation to judges and magistrates on behalf of a client who has been convicted but not yet sentenced. But not all criminal lawyers are involved in defence. There are also opportunities for prosecution lawyers.

The main employer of prosecution lawyers is the Crown Prosecution Service with an establishment of around 2,500 lawyers. However many local authority and other regulatory organisations also employ prosecution lawyers to deal with specific areas of work. Criminal law solicitors are represented by the Criminal Law Solicitors Association.

Personal Injury Claims

You may have heard many radio adverts asking, "Have you been injured in an accident which wasn't your fault?"

You know immediately that the advertisement has been

placed by a personal injury claims lawyer. They want you to know that, if you have suffered such an accident, they can fight your claim without risk or expense to yourself, safe in the knowledge that their costs will be paid by the insurers of the person who caused the accident. With the roll back in civil legal aid, the bulk of personal injury litigation is now conducted on the basis of no-win-no-fee. It is different from the contingency fee arrangements which apply in the USA because UK lawyers do not take a chunk of the damages. And because most claims, where the defendant is insured, now settle before they come to trial, the risk for the lawyer is perhaps not as great as you might think. Personal injury claims commonly cover accidents at work, road accidents, and public liability. The last covers everything where an innocent member of public suffers injury as a result of somebody else's fault. An example might be somebody slipping on a wet floor or who gets in the way of a falling object.

Under no-win-no fee, the client pays only if they win the case. They will sign an agreement to that effect. It means that the lawyer then takes the risk as to whether the case is won or lost. If the case is lost, the lawyer gets paid nothing for their work. If the client wins, they will be paid a bit extra to cover the risk they have taken in agreeing to pursue the claim. What is crucial for a no-win-no-fee lawyer is that they know a good case when they see one.

As well as claims-lawyers there also need to be personal injury defence lawyers. Their clients will normally be the insurers of the party which is alleged to have caused the accident.

Insurance work is undoubtedly safer because the lawyer will be paid win-or-lose. But they will be working to specifically negotiated rates agreed with the insurer. Claimant personal injury lawyers are represented by the 2,900 strong Nottingham based Association of Personal Injury Lawyers (APIL).

General Litigation

This will cover all civil litigation not included in any of the specialist categories listed above. It is sometimes referred to as 'Common Law' because the basics of civil law developed over the centuries on a case-by-case basis, supplemented by statute as the need arises. The work-place for the civil litigator is the High Court, the county courts, the Court of Appeal and the Supreme Court. Amongst the most basic work of the civil litigator is the pursuance of money claims, from the £10,000 small-claims limit upwards. At a higher level such claims could extend to mortgage possessions. Other work might include injunction proceedings to stop an actual or threatened infringement of a client's rights.

The work of the general litigation lawyer involves the drafting and issue of legal proceedings; preparation of witness statements; pre-trial disclosure; and advocacy at the trial itself – if in fact no settlement is reached beforehand. But getting a judgment against a client's opponent may not be the end of the matter. The hard part may be enforcing that judgment. The law offers a range of options for enforcing a judgement: from bailiffs, attachment of earnings, or freezing a bank account –

though to bankruptcy and company liquidation. Not much use though if a debtor has no money or other assets to attach. It is why the outcome of any litigation can never be guaranteed.

Company and Commercial

Undoubtedly one the highest paid of all legal work and one which has an international dimension. It covers everything from mergers and acquisitions; company formation and re-structuring; business transfers; commercial contracts; trademarks; patents and copyright. A company lawyer must know how to set up and dissolve companies and understand the statutory responsibilities which apply to directors. A company lawyer must also have a sufficient knowledge of intellectual property (which includes copyright, trademarks, patents and associated protections) to enable the company to protect its research and development. Company lawyers also require a specific understanding of the particular industry within which their client-company operates. The oil and gas industry provides an obvious example. And they must also be comfortable sitting at a directors' board meeting. Another major aspect of a company lawyer's work is 'compliance'.

'Compliance' means the need for the company to comply with regulatory processes: both generally and specifically within the industry within which the company operates. This includes compliance with legislation applicable to all trading companies, such as the filing of annual returns and financial information. Key to any business is the need to comply with the Data

Protection Act 1998, which means that anyone systematically holding information about private living individuals must register with the Information Commissioner and to have processes in place to ensure that such personal information is kept securely and used only for the express purposes for which it has been obtained. So what happens if the company's IT systems are hacked and personal information ends up in the hands of criminals? Where will the liabilities fall? It may be the company lawyer who has to limit the damage. 'Compliance' applicable to the finance industry means registration with the Financial Conduct Authority and adherence to rules to prevent money-laundering. For solicitors, 'compliance' means carrying out to the letter the requirements of the SRA handbook.

Company work is international in the sense that commerce does not respect national boundaries. Lawyers working for the largest companies may be regularly travelling to the world's furthest outposts. Even the company itself may be registered overseas. Companies may be registered in any jurisdiction and still be able to own assets and trade within the UK. Company lawyers may work as the in-house counsel of large public companies. Or they may work for private law firms with company clients. Company lawyers are represented within the Law Society by the Commerce and Industry Group.

Public Law

Public law is the term given to the decision making processes of public sector organisations, such as local councils, the NHS, the police, fire service and other regulatory bodies including Government Ministers, the Solicitors Regulation Authority and the Bar Standards Board. It is sometime called 'civil rights' because of the effect the decisions of such organisations have on the rights of private individuals. Public law has developed through a string of decided cases stretching back to 1947. Public law is not so much concerned with the actual decision reached, as with the process by which a decision is reached. It is only if the decision-makers have not approached the process in a lawful and rational manner, that the decision will be set aside. Since 1998 judges have also been required to take account of the Human Rights issues in determining whether decisions have been properly made.

The battleground for the public law lawyer is the Administrative Court. Their chief weapon is the application for Judicial Review, in which they ask a High Court Judge to review the lawfulness of the way in which a decision was made. If the court decides that there were irregularities in that decision-making process, it can revoke the decision and direct the decision-making body to look at the matter again and make a new decision on the basis of correct legal principles.

Niche Work

Most lawyers practicing in the UK will work in one or more of the mainstream practice areas listed above. But there are some 'niche' practice areas which are so specialist that there may be only a few hundred lawyers with that expertise. Here are some examples:

• Media lawyers – who act for the newspaper, radio, television and on-line entertainment industries. They are expert in the laws of libel and slander and in the management of risk. They might be asked to advise on a specific news-story or opinion-piece before it is even published.

• Child care lawyers – predominantly employed by larger local authorities with social-care responsibilities. Arguably one of the most stressful lawyer-jobs as it involves a requirement to act quickly – and at any time of the day or night – to protect a child's safety. However there are some who work in private practise. Child care lawyers are represented by the Association of Child Care Lawyers. As well as child care lawyers, there are also lawyers specializing in education law and adult social-care.

• Planning and Development Lawyers. Most local authorities with town planning responsibilities will retain a small team of planning lawyers to defend their councils' planning decisions and also to negotiate with developers' lawyers on legally binding schemes to govern the process of any major development. Developers will also use lawyers to assist in putting together a site for redevelopment. Many areas of land which have become ripe for redevelopment are in many different ownerships. It is then the job of the development lawyer to 'assemble' the site like a jigsaw until it is within a single ownership. Only then can it be redeveloped. Once the estate has been developed it then falls to other lawyers to handle individual 'plot sales' to the end buyers. The job of a development lawyer also include the negotiation and documentation of arrangements with the local planning authority and public utility companies to enable the grant of planning permission and ensure that the finished development is adequately serviced with drainage, water, gas and electricity. Planning Lawyers who can demonstrate sufficient expertise can qualify as Associates of the Royal Town Planning Institute.

Chapter Eleven

WHAT MAKES A LAWYER

In this chapter we look at the personal qualities which every lawyer must have and the reasons why those personal qualities are so important. They are ranked in descending order of importance. Here they are.

Integrity

So much of modern legal practice is based on trust. If banks could not trust lawyers to look after their money, the whole conveyancing system would grind to a halt. Nobody would be able to buy or sell property. Witnesses may lie but judges and magistrates have to be able to trust the word of the advocate who stands in front of them. Lawyers on opposite sides in a court case may each be fighting to win but at the same time they have to be able to trust each other to play by the rules. It is why integrity is right at the top of the list when the Solicitors' Regulation Authority or any other professional body assesses somebody's fitness to be a lawyer. If one lawyer cheats it can undermine public confidence in the entire profession. So what does integrity mean?

It means more than not being dishonest. It's about strength of character. It's about determination to do the right thing, whatever the personal cost. It means being prepared to refuse a client's instructions rather than bow to pressure to do something which is not quite right. Easy enough! You might think. There are plenty of other clients. But suppose that the client who wants you to compromise your integrity is the one who provides 60% of your business? Not so easy.

The importance of integrity is recognized in the full title of a solicitor, which is 'Solicitor of the Senior Courts of England and Wales.' Until 2009 the title was 'Solicitor of the Supreme Court'. But when the Judicial Committee of the House of Lords was itself renamed as the Supreme Court, a new title had to be found. It means that whatever a client may want, a solicitor's first duty is to the administration of justice.

Being Streetwise

Being streetwise goes hand-in-hand with integrity. It is a dangerous world out there. You are now more likely to be mugged on the internet than in the street. And one of the biggest threats to the wallet is conveyancing fraud. It's a billion dollar industry. The crime is one of impersonation.

Typically someone will dupe a lawyer into thinking that they own a property which belongs to someone else. It will usually be an empty property or one which is tenanted. They will have already found out from the Land Registry the name and address of the rightful owner and will pretend that they are that person. They may even produce forged papers to convince the lawyer that they are whom they pretend.

The lawyer then acts on the 'sale'. The buyer's lawyer assumes that the seller's lawyer has carried out all due diligence checks as to the seller's bona fides and pays the completion monies into the seller's lawyer's client account. Following completion of the sale, the seller's lawyer passes on the completion money to the bogus seller, who disappears into the night. Then the rightful owner turns up and demands that the property is returned to them. So who picks up the £500,000 bill?

Well it can't be the buyer's lawyer because they are entitled to rely on you, as the Seller's lawyer, to have made sure that you are acting for the rightful owner. They have done everything correctly. You're the one who has been duped. So it is down to you – or your insurer – to make good the loss. Well that was the position until January 2017, when in the case of Dreamvar (UK) Limited v Mishcon de Reya, [2016] 3316 (Ch), the High Court ruled that buyer's lawyers, Mishcons, were liable for a £1.1M 'owner' fraud, even though they had followed good conveyancing practice to the letter.

It seems that the judge was more influenced by Mishcon's generous insurance policy than the absence of error on their part. And there is another more sophisticated version of this fraud in which the fraudster impersonates an entire conveyancing firm. This fraud is about duping the buyer's lawyer.

You as the buyer's lawyer will be dealing with a reputable conveyancing firm which is acting for the seller. Or at least you think you are. Let's call them Buggs Brown Solicitors (apologies to any real solicitors of that name). They correspond with you using a Buggs Brown letterhead. Only the letterhead is a forgery. The person you are dealing with isn't a real Buggs Brown solicitor: they are a fraudster. Eventually you pay £500,000 to Buggs Brown's client account to complete the 'purchase'. Only it's not a real solicitors' client account. The money disappears off into to the ether. Title to the property is not transferred. The real Bugs Brown know nothing about the transaction. You have been conned.

A third fraud is where a fraudster hacks into lawyer's computer system and sends out emails to clients and other solicitors pretending that the firm's bank details have been changed. Money intended for the solicitors' firm will then be transmitted instead by those clients to the fraudster's account. It is why, to cover themselves, law firms now routinely warn clients and third parties not to be taken in by bogus emails notifying them of changed account details.

Being streetwise means being alert to the tiniest clues which indicate that something is not quite right. Maybe there is undue haste to complete the transaction. Maybe the client doesn't want to see you and acts through intermediaries. Maybe there are spelling mistakes or use of strange terminology in correspondence and emails.

Being Meticulous

When preparing legal documentation, errors and omissions will be expensive. Imagine preparing a residential ground-lease which reserves an annual ground-rent of £10,000 instead the nominal £100 which the parties intended. If the client or the other party spots the mistake before signing the document, it can be corrected. But supposing they don't? Supposing it is another ten years down the line when a new landlord looks at the lease and wonders why they are only receiving £100 from the leaseholder instead of the £10,000 which the lease states should be paid. There is a dispute.

There is also a tendency for modern judges to interpret the terms of a document literally even when those stated terms do not make any commercial sense. So if the lease says £10,000, then that is what the leaseholder is going to pay. It does not matter that no residential leaseholder in their right mind would agree to pay an annual £10,000 ground-rent for a flat which they own outright. Even if the typo is spotted in good time and corrected it still undermines client confidence in your competence to look after their interests. Someone who is paying you £200 an hour should not also have to act as your spellchecker.

Being a People Person

Like the late actor, George Cole, you may exude an old world charm to which the rest of the world warms. For everyone else there's Dale Carnegie's 'How to Win Friends and Influence People'. Yes – it's true. Human relationships are a skill which can be learned. And Carnegie was its greatest teacher. The rules are pretty basic.

It's about taking a genuine interest in people and the world around you. It's about looking outwards. It is about taking the trouble to remember somebody's name. It is about showing that you are pleased to see someone. It is about making that person feel valued. It is about understanding what is important to that person. It's about never putting someone down. It's about offering sincere appreciation to someone: never flattery. And of course you will never be tempted to openly criticize someone or complain. And it doesn't matter whether that person is a sharp-suited businessman – or woman – or a prisoner in a cell. The rules are the same.

The law is a people-profession. It is all about how you interact with your clients; prospective clients; the lawyer on the other side; the judge or magistrate who is sitting in front of you – and all the people in between. Don't like meeting people? Then go and be an accountant. Or drive a tube train. But don't be a lawyer. Because meeting people is what the law is all about.

Being Passionate About Your Work

As we saw in the first chapter, what all celebrity lawyers have in common is that they are passionate about their work. If they were not passionate, they would not have been able to develop the expertise and the niche on which their fame depends. If you are not passionate about the law and becoming a lawyer, don't even take the first step. Find something else which you are passionate about. If you are not passionate about becoming a lawyer, you may not even make it through to qualification. And if you do, what sort of average legal career will you carve out for yourself? Passion is the inner motivator. If you are passionate about your career, you will master all of the other skills and qualities which make a good lawyer.

Being a Good Communicator

This goes hand-in-hand with being a people person. If you don't have a genuine liking for people, how are you going to communicate with them?

Barristers have to be good on their feet and able to command a room. They have to be able to respond instantly to any situation. They can't clam up. They must also be able to express themselves in writing and in the drafting of court documents. All solicitors must be able to communicate effectively on a one-to-one basis both verbally and in writing. If they can command a room as well: that is a bonus. But like people-skills: verbal and written communication are things which can be learned.

If you want to be confident on your feet, join a public speaking club. It is cheap and you will be practicing week-in week-out in a supportive environment. Toastmasters International are the brand-leader. It was founded more than a century ago in Bloomington, Illinois by Ralph Smedley. As Director of Education for the YMCA he saw the need for men to be able to speak, conduct meetings, plan programmes and work on committees. That was in 1905. It was almost seven decades later that Toastmasters officially opened up its meetings to women. The organisation now has branches in every City in the World. Until the late 1980s there was only one Toastmasters Club in London, which met fortnightly at the US Navy Building at Grosvenor Square. That Club still exists under the name 'Grosvenor Square Toastmasters Club' even though it now meets at the New Cavendish Club in Marble Arch. Dozens more Clubs have since joined it.

Every Toastmasters' meeting begins with an impromptu 'topics' session in which members are picked out of the audience and given random topics on which to speak for up to two minutes. Its purpose is to help participants to 'think-on-their-feet'. The second half of the evening starts with prepared speeches. All speeches, whether impromptu or prepared, receive constructive feedback and encouragement. Unfortunately there are as yet no clubs for written communication. Yes – every town has its Writers Circles. But those are for people who want to write stories not compose business correspondence.

Business writing is something which has to be learned solo. Forget the essays which you wrote at school. Business writing is different. It has its own rules which have more in common with the secrets of selling than artistic impression. It is about getting a point across: whether that point is to inform the reader about a state of affairs or to persuade the reader to take a course of action – such as paying an outstanding bill. Whilst there are books on business letter writing, it is a skill which can only be fully learned by doing. And of course by developing your own business style.

Start by looking at other peoples' business correspondence. Try to spot the differences between something which is well-written and persuasive - and something which is incoherent and meaningless. It is said that, 'the pen is mightier than the sword'. But not if the writing is littered with typos and an incoherent message. What the phrase means is that a well written letter carries power. It achieves results. Look for a piece of writing which is so good you want to frame it. Then break it down.

Look at the structure of the letter and how it gets its point across. How does the letter open? Why was it written? How does it convince the reader? And what is it asking the reader to do? Use it as your template. Then practice writing a similar letter of your own. Even though traditional letter writing has largely given way to text and email, the principles are the same. But email and text will never supplant letter-writing completely.

There is a time and a place for email and text. They are informal and chatty. But in the law there will always be a need for more formal written communication. Only a letter can provide that formality. Within the legal profession there are also conventions to be observed when lawyers communicate with other lawyers, third parties and with clients. They all require an element of detachment. Disregard those conventions and you may seen as 'unprofessional'.

A client expects a lawyer to look and communicate like a lawyer. If they are paying £100 for a 45 minute consultation, they want to see somebody in a suit. They want to be addressed as Mr and Mrs Jones – not Bob and Angie. If they see somebody dressed in jeans and a tee-shirt they will feel cheated. When lawyers write to each other or to a third party, many still use the Royal 'We' as in, *"We are acting for..."*. The 'We' may change to the more personal 'I' when the lawyer writes to their own client: but not always. But the form of communication which many lawyers find most difficult is networking.

Remember that for a lawyer in private practice, it is not just about doing the work. It also about getting the work. Why should a prospective client bring their work to you instead of the other solicitor who works down the road? It's not just about you being the cheapest. If you are someone whom they already know and you can inspire them with confidence, they are more likely to instruct you.

One way of getting to know prospective business clients is through networking. It is about being able to walk into a large room full of strangers and engage with at least some of them. It requires all your skills as a people-person and as an effective communicator. You are not, 'working the room'. You are not selling anything except yourself. But if can you can come away from the network event with at least one new business contact, it has been a success. But that is only the start. Contacts have to be followed up. Like people-skills, networking is something which can be learned. Practice it.

Being Able to Think Creatively

So much of the law is about process: whether it is following through a conveyancing transaction or defending a criminal prosecution. Anyone can follow process. But what makes a lawyer is the ability to see beyond the process and use it to get the result which your client needs – or as near as possible. Think about the problem questions which you did at school. Thinking creatively is about analyzing a situation, knowing what questions to ask, identifying options and then being able to provide a client with a clear and reasoned recommendation as to what option would be right for them.

Being Able to Work at Speed

Suppose your normal hourly charge-out rate is £200. By quoting your client a flat fee of £1,000 for acting on the purchase of their house, you are gambling on the transaction not taking more than five hours of your time. If it takes ten hours of your time, your hourly charge-out is effectively reduced to £100 and your firm will bear the loss and you will not meet your yearly target.

It is why it is important to be able to turn work around quickly. No-one wants a slow lawyer. Not clients. They don't want to have to keep chasing or to worry about the deal falling through. Not estate agents, whose commission structure means that they only get paid when the transaction completes.

Working quickly doesn't mean cutting corners. What it does mean is an ability to organize your day efficiently and make best use of your time and the resources which are available to you. It means learning how to delegate, assuming that there is someone to whom you can delegate. Speed should also come with experience, once you have got a 'feel' for the process. It is why the most junior lawyer in the firm may not be the most economic for the client if it takes them twice as long to do the job.

Chapter Twelve

HOW TO QUALIFY AS A SOLICITOR

As the first draft of this chapter was being written, the process of qualifying as a solicitor was under review by the Solicitors Regulation Authority (SRA). However any replacement of the current qualification process is not expected to take place until September 2020. Even then there will be transitional arrangements enabling anyone who has already started their journey towards qualification to qualify under the existing procedures if they wish to do so. For the purposes of this chapter we will provide a detailed account of the qualification process as it exists at present and an overview of the changes which are expected to take place in 2020.

In December 2015 the SRA began its consultation process into how the qualification process might be reformed and a year later (December 2016) published worked up proposals for a new Solicitors Qualifying Examination to replace the Legal

Practice Course (see below). Those worked up proposals went through a second round of consultation and in April 2017 the SRA confirmed the structure of the proposed changes. In some respects those changes will take the qualification process back to where it was in the 1970s before it became a graduate only profession but introducing a new regulated assessment of practical solicitor-skills.

Before the profession became graduate only, it was possible for a school-leaver with at least two A Levels to qualify as a solicitor via a five-year sandwich course. It began with a year-long course at the College of Law followed by the Law Society's Part I Examination. Passing Part 1 meant that the candidate could then seek a four year training contract (then known as Articles of Clerkship) with a solicitors' firm: and there were plenty to choose from. It seemed that every firm of solicitors from the largest to the sole practitioners had their articled clerks.

Even when the profession became graduate only during the 1980s, going – or not going – to university was still a matter of choice for any school-leaver who had the required A level grades. The fact that a university education was state funded, with additional living allowances meant that no-one was denied a university education simply because their family could not afford it. Unfortunately that is no longer the case.

At the very same time that a university degree has become an essential passport for almost any worthwhile career, successive Government policies have made it unaffordable for many people. With annual tuition fees of £9,000 and rising, cost has become the new factor for anyone deciding their career options. Yes – there are student loans. And – No -it doesn't have to be paid until your income reaches a certain threshold. But it will still have to be paid – even if not immediately. And then you have to pay to keep yourself during the three years when you will not be earning any money. Fortunately this particular graduate-only profession has never been completely graduate only. There are currently two categories of non-graduate solicitors, namely:

+ Those who had already qualified – or who were already in the process of qualification – at the point the profession became graduate-only during the 1980s;

+ Former Legal Executives who have upgraded their qualifications to become solicitors, even though they did not require a university degree to become Legal Executives. Around 25% of solicitors still qualify in this way.

There is now a third way in which a person can become a solicitor without going to university: that is to take the new Legal Apprenticeship route. This new route gets round the graduate issue by requiring apprentices to acquire legal knowledge equivalent to someone who has gone to university and gained a degree. But the beauty of the apprenticeship is that you don't actually have to take three years out to go to university. So you can learn while you learn. Overall it will take just as long to qualify as a solicitor though the apprenticeship route and you won't have the letters after your name. But neither will you have collected at £27,000 debt.

The other issue which the SRA is having to address is training contracts: which currently is the biggest barrier to qualification. There is only so much you can learn out of books. They will tell you the law, the procedures and the process of interviewing a client. But how you apply that knowledge is down to you. It comes with experience. It is not just about knowing the law and procedures: it is also about getting a 'feel' for them. That 'feel' can only come if you have actually worked in a solicitors' office. It is why the current qualification process requires a would-be solicitor to have spent at least two years dealing with supervised legal work within a solicitors' office. And that on-the-job training requirement will continue when new training regulations take effect in 2020 but with greater choice as to how that training is obtained. The current problem is that training contracts are a buyers' market.

There are more candidates wanting training contracts then there are contracts available. It is a competitive market. It means that every year there are a significant numbers of candidates who have passed all the academic stages of the qualifying process but who cannot go on to become solicitors because they cannot get training contracts. However this is not a barrier for Legal Executives wanting to upgrade their qualification, to the extent that they can demonstrate that they already have sufficient on-the-job experience. Neither is it a barrier to legal apprentices: whose on-the-job training extends throughout the length of their apprenticeship. The competition for apprentices comes at the beginning, with the scramble for a limited number of apprenticeship places – not at the end when you have invested £42,000 and at least four years of your life getting a law degree and completing the Legal Practice Course. And all on the gamble that you will eventually get a training contract. Under the existing qualifying regime there are six different ways in which someone can qualify as a solicitor:

◆ By obtaining a Qualifying Law Degree, followed by the Legal Practice Course (LPC), two years recognized training and a Professional Skills Course (PSC). This is the mainstream route to qualification and takes around six years to qualify at an average overall cost of £42,000;

◆ By converting a non-law degree to something which the SRA recognizes by passing a Common Professional Examination (CPE) (also known as the Graduate Diploma in Law) followed by the LPC, two years recognized training and PSC. Takes on average seven years to qualify at an overall cost of £51,000.

◆ By upgrading Fellowship of the Chartered Institute of Legal Executives (CILEX).

◆ Under the Qualified Lawyers Transfer Scheme, which enables lawyers already qualified in other jurisdictions to convert their qualifications.

◆ By Equivalent Means – whereby a person is able to demonstrate that they have acquired knowledge, skills and practical experience at least equivalent to that which they would have obtained by following a more conventional route to qualification.

• Through the new Apprenticeship Route where legal knowledge and skill derives from workplace experience, with a Synoptic End Point Assessment. Estimated time to qualify is six years.

Later in this chapter we will look at each of these options in depth. But there are some important SRA documents which govern the whole of any solicitors qualification process and more besides. The first of these is the SRA Handbook, which is the Bible of the Solicitors Profession. Although it is called a 'Handbook' it is in fact an on-line resource which is frequently updated and covers everything from ethics, through to the protection of clients, the holding of client money – and of course training and qualification requirements. These are referred to simply as the Training Regulations 2014. Google 'SRA Handbook' and log on to it. It is your first point of reference for anything to do with the solicitors profession. The Law Society Book Shop also sells the SRA Handbook as a paperback. The Handbook is stated to be 'outcomes focused': which means that the SRA is more concerned with having a solicitors' profession which is trustworthy and provides a good quality of service, rather than setting out detailed regulations and processes. The word 'outcomes' is also used in defining the qualification process. It doesn't really matter how you get there so long as at the point of qualification you have sufficient grounding in legal knowledge and technical skills to do your job.

On 11th March 2015 the SRA published a 'Statement of Solicitor Competence', being 'the ability to perform the roles and tasks required by one's job to the expected standard'. The document is to be read together with a 'Threshold Standard' and a 'Statement of Legal Knowledge' and is being used to produce the new assessment framework for admission to the profession. The Competency Statement runs to nine pages but in summary sets standards for:

- Ethics, professionalism and judgement;
- Technical Legal Practice;
- Working with other people;
- Self-management.

Download the document and compare its requirements with the essential lawyer qualities listed in the previous chapter. Then download the next document which is the Threshold Standard, which is set out in the form of a grid and which distinguishes (in five levels) the extent to which a solicitor should meet each of the listed competencies at the point of qualification. Each Level is split into six columns, namely: Functioning Legal Knowledge; Standard of Work; Autonomy; Complexity; Perception of Context; Innovation and Originality.

The bare minimum for a newly qualified solicitor is Level 3, which means (in terms of Autonomy) that the person 'Achieves most tasks and able to progress legal matters using own judgement, recognizing when support is needed'. But compare this with Level 5, where the newly qualified, 'Takes full responsibility for outcomes of case or transaction.' It is these thresholds which will govern the standard of future legal examinations and the number of marks required to pass. The third document in the trilogy is the Statement of Legal Knowledge, which will guide the content of future solicitor training and qualification. It sets out the breadth of knowledge which solicitors are required to demonstrate at the point of qualification. In summary these comprise:

♦ Ethics, professional conduct and regulation including money laundering and solicitors accounts;

♦ Wills and administration of estates;

♦ Taxation (namely: income tax; capital gains tax corporation tax; value added tax).

♦ The law of organizations. In other words 'Company Law' but also covering the newer Limited Liability Partnerships.

♦ Freehold and leasehold conveyancing

♦ Torts (meaning non-criminal wrongs) but limited to negligence and related areas; assault; defamation; damages and injunctions.

♦ Criminal law and procedure

♦ Contract law

♦ Trusts

♦ Constitutional Law and EU law (including Human Rights)

♦ The Legal System of England and Wales

♦ Civil Litigation

This list provides no more than a snapshot of a mountain of laws and legal principles stretching back centuries. But mastery of these selected topics will suffice for legal qualification. Other mainstream areas of law such as Family or Consumer Law do not even get a mention. We now look in more detail at the options for qualification as they exist at present.

The Mainstream Route to Qualification as a Solicitor

The mainstream route for solicitor-qualification is a university degree. That degree does not have to be in the law. But if you successfully complete a Qualifying Law Degree (QLD) you can move straight on to the Legal Practice Course, which is the final part of the examination process. But to complete the qualification process you will also need at least two years of supervised training within a law office. If you have a degree which is not a QLD, you will need to pass a one year post-graduate conversion course known as the Common Professional Examination (or Graduate Diploma in Law). Whilst QLDs and CPEs can be studied full or part-time or by distance learning, the SRA has set out time limits within which the degree-course must be completed. The good news is that QLDs and CPEs are a gateway not only for the solicitors' profession but also for barristers. So it is possible to change course during this initial period of qualification. We now look at QLDs and CPEs in more detail.

In July 2014 the SRA and the Bar Standards Board jointly produced the Academic Stage Handbook (ASH) which sets out the requirements for a QLD and CPE and the time-limits within which they must be passed. The SRA also publishes a list of universities providing these qualifications. Whilst the SRA/BSB specify the core outcomes which a QLD/CPE must achieve, each university will have its own variants for getting there and as regards assessment. But the ASH states that for a QLD the study of legal subjects must be not less than two years out of a four year course of study. This is because legal knowledge becomes stale because the law is changing so fast. From 1st September 2011 the maximum time for completion of a QLD (whether full or part-time or by distance learning) is six years. The maximum number of attempts for the Foundations of Legal Knowledge subjects (see below) is three. The content of a QLD must include the Foundations of Legal Knowledge, which are described as:

- Public law, including Constitutional Law, Administrative Law and Human Rights
  - Law of the European Union
  - Criminal Law
  - Obligations including Contract, Restitution and Tort
  - Property Law
  - Equity and the Law of Trusts.

In addition to the Foundations the QLD must also provide students with training in legal research. Students sitting the CPE must also pass the same Foundations of Legal Knowledge as for the QLD but with one other area of legal study. The CPE is an intense, condensed programme of study specifically designed for graduates or students with equivalent qualifications. The time-limits for the CPE is from 1 to 3 years (full time) or 2 to 4 years (part time). The maximum number of attempts for each CPE subject is three, failing which they are required to re-take a full CPE course. Before leaving degrees and conversion courses it is worth mentioning two enhanced courses, namely:

* An Exempting Law Degree (ELD), which combines QLDs with an LPC (see below);
* An Integrated Course (IC), which combines the Foundations of Legal Knowledge with an LPC.

Look on the internet for universities offering ELDs or ICs. The final examination stage in the mainstream process is the Legal Practice Course, which again is outcomes focused

The Legal Practice Course (LPC) is the final examination stage in the mainstream route to solicitor-qualification. If you make it to this stage you will have already learned the Seven Foundations of Legal Knowledge gained either via a QLD or the CPE. The SRA have stated what the LPC should achieve in 'Legal Practice Course Outcomes 2011, which can be downloaded from the Internet. It is around that central specification that each university offering the LPC has designed its course. The LPC is in two Stages.

Stage 1 comprises the following:

* Professional Conduct and Regulation, namely: the core requirements of integrity, trustworthiness, independence, an understanding of the SRA Code of Conduct and how

it is applied, anti-money laundering and financial services regulation, Solicitors Accounts.

♦ Wills and Estates, namely a general overview of the content, format and validity of wills, how to obtain probate or letters of administration relating to a deceased person's estate, how to collect together the assets and deal with any claims against the estate and how it is distributed to the beneficiaries.

♦ Taxation, and how it impacts on other areas covered by the LPC, with particular reference to: Income Tax, Capital Gains Tax, Inheritance Tax, Corporation Tax and VAT.

♦ Business Law and Practice (being one of the three Core Practice Areas), including the ability to progress basic business transactions arising during the life and development of a business including the drafting of relevant documentation. Candidates will know how to set up companies and advise clients on their advantages and disadvantages; entering into contracts; the borrowing of money; shareholders and issues related to insolvency;

♦ Property Law and Practice (the second Core Practice Area): which means that the candidate should be able to process a typical conveyancing transaction (freehold and leasehold)and look after a client's interests as well as the interests of mortgage lenders.

♦ Litigation (the third Core Practice Area), which covers both civil and criminal litigation and includes: evaluation of evidence, the several ways in which litigation is funded; and civil and criminal procedure.

♦ Course Skills – namely: oral and written communication

across a range of media including document drafting, interviewing and advising clients, presentations and the need to demonstrate sensitivity to issues of culture, diversity and disability; practical legal research involving legal and factual issues, identification and application of relevant case-law, statute and regulations using paper and electronic search tools and the presentation of conclusions and recommendations; attention to detail; awareness of practical, commercial and personal considerations to be taken into account, recognition of any Conduct issues and the need to act within the Code of Conduct

Stage 2 of the LPC involves a student's choice of three vocational electives from the range offered by the particular university at which the course is being taken. At the end of each elective the student should be able to demonstrate their understanding of and their ability to apply what they have learned from the elective; identify a client's goals and then plan and progress a transaction including the drafting of relevant documentation. The following is an example of LPC Electives offered by The City Law School: Equity Finance; Commercial Law; Advanced Civil Litigation, Employment law; Family Law; Mergers and Acquisitions; Commercial Dispute Resolution; Private Client; Media law.

You've now got your Qualifying Law Degree and you've passed the Legal Practice Course. Congratulations! You've done the easy part. Now to complete the qualification process to become a solicitor you need a two year Period of Recognised Training. Yes – that's the new name for the Training Contract.

It is a supervised opportunity for you to apply what you've learned at university and on the LPC. And also to gain the soft skills which you will need to work as a solicitor. But the process is competitive.

Imagine applying for a job in which you are competing against twelve other candidates. Only one of you can get it. Even though you may be the most qualified and able candidate, that doesn't guarantee that you'll get the job. It all depends on how you sell yourself in your CV. And how you connect on the day. The process is subjective.

Are you projecting the right attitude? How well will you fit into the organization? Will you be easy to work with? Does your manner inspire confidence? Are you worth the investment which the firm will make in employing and training you? It's all about impression.

In her article 'How to: Get a Training Contract', which was published in the Law Society Gazette on 8th September 2014, Mondipa Fouzder refers to 17,500 law students and only 5,000 training contracts. Later in this chapter we will provide some tips on getting a training contract. We will also show you what you can do if you are one of those who have missed out on getting a training contract. The good news is that your qualifications have not been wasted. There are other routes into the profession. But first we look at what a Period of Recognised Training (PRT) entails.

Download the SRA Trainee Information Pack, which sets out everything you need to know about Recognised Training. Before starting Training you must first notify the SRA of your intention to do so using a form which can be downloaded from the internet. As well as having met the academic requirements, there is also a Suitability Test, to ensure that any individual seeking admission as a solicitor has and maintains the level of honesty, integrity and professionalism which the public is entitled to expect and does not pose a risk to the public or the solicitors' profession. The test applies the same high standards to anyone seeking admission as already applies to someone who is legally qualified. When notifying the SRA of their intention to undertake a PRT, all applicants are required to confirm either that there have been no issues as regards their character or to disclose to the SRA what those issues are. If there are disclosed character issues the SRA will decide whether to allow PRT according to the following criteria.

Save where there are exceptional circumstances, the SRA will always refuse an application where the candidate has been convicted of a criminal offence where: the candidate has received a custodial or suspended sentence; an offence involving dishonesty, fraud, perjury or bribery; which has resulted in the candidate being entered on the Violent and Sex Offender Register; is associated with obstructing the course of justice; involves some form of unlawful discrimination; involves a repeat offence; or is otherwise so serious as to make a PRT inappropriate.

The SRA are *more likely than not* to refuse an application if the candidate: has been convicted of an offence (not triggering automatic disqualification) but which still impacts on the candidate's character and suitability; involves inclusion on

111

the Violent and Sex Offenders' Register but not as a result of a criminal conviction; or involves a police caution for an offence involving dishonesty.

The SRA *may* refuse an application if the candidate: has received a local warning from the police; has accepted a police caution for an offence not involving dishonesty; or involves receipt of a Penalty Notice for Disorder from the police.

When there is a criminal offence, police caution or penalty notice, the SRA will not question the finding of guilt but will take into account any sentencing remarks or independent information. Candidates are also required to disclose any criminal charges which are pending, in which case the SRA will not determine the application until the outcome of the proceedings are known. Candidates are also warned not to accept police cautions lightly as they themselves are an admission of guilt. Penalty Notices are different as payment discharges the risk of conviction. However they must still be disclosed. Even motoring convictions (although not the accumulation of penalty points) must be disclosed.

Everyone seeking admission as a solicitor is required to apply for standard disclosure from the Disclosure and Barring Service. Any failure to disclose material information is itself treated as evidence of dishonesty. But it is not just clear-cut criminal behavior which can disqualify a candidate from getting a training contract.

In the absence of exceptional circumstances the SRA will disqualify a candidate for any behaviour which is: dishonest;, violent, involves discrimination, misuse of a position to obtain financial advantage; misuse of a position of trust in relation to vulnerable people or other behaviour which demonstrates that the candidate cannot be relied upon to carry out their regulatory duties as a solicitor. Other disqualifying circumstances include plagiarism or cheating in an examination; an inability to manage one's financial affairs, which will be presumed from the existence of any county court judgment or bankruptcy; or other disciplinary finding, sanction or action by any regulatory body. Where a disclosure has to be made and to help the SRA to deal with it the SRA requests that the candidate also provides: one independent report relating to the event; references from two independent professional people; evidence of any rehabilitation. Let's now assume that you have satisfied the Suitability Test and are able to start your Period of Recognised Training.

The Training Contract itself constitutes an apprenticeship contract of employment between the trainee and their employer. This is not to be confused with new stand-alone apprenticeship route to qualification which is described below. But the Training Contract is still an apprenticeship in the eyes of the law, which means that the employer can only terminate it in the event of serious misconduct, or if the candidate is so incapacitated as to be incapable of being trained or where the business has closed or fundamentally changed.

The PRT gives trainees a supervised opportunity to develop and apply their practice skills through their own work, by assisting others and observing experienced practitioners. On completion of their training, it is expected that candidates will be competent to exercise those rights of audience before courts and tribunals which are available to a newly qualified solicitor. It means that they will have the ability to communicate as an advocate, understand the tactics of cross-examination and the need to act in accordance with the ethics, etiquette and conventions of the professional advocate. They will also know how to manage their own time, effort and available resources. They will also need the opportunity to develop other written and oral communication skills through: drafting correspondence and more formal documentation; reporting to clients and taking meeting notes. They will also need to know how to resolve a dispute in the most cost-effective and timely way, whether through settlement , negotiation, mediation or third-party adjudication. And they need to be given tasks which involve finding solutions through research – both on-line and paper-based. It is also worth mentioning that it is not only candidates who require permission to start PRT. Any law firm which wishes to offer training contracts also requires authorisation from the SRA. And the criteria is strict. The requirements are that trainees must:

- Be paid at least the National Minimum Wage.Recommended trainee salaries are slightly more;
- Be given experience in at least three distinct areas of law – if necessary by offering the trainee secondment to another organization if the firm cannot provide that variety directly,
- Give trainees the opportunities they need to develop the skills they need in the contentious and non-contentious work to meet the Practice Skills Standard;

◆ Maintain a training record;

◆ Work under the supervision of qualified solicitors or others with appropriate legal experience;

◆ Receive regular feedback and appraisals throughout their training;

◆ Successfully complete the professional Skills Course (see below).

How long a PRT lasts depends on how many days a week the trainee works. For a full time trainee the period is two years. Someone working 2.5 days a week would have to train for four years. For someone working four days a week the period would be two years and six months. The training period can be reduced where a trainee has previously worked in a legal environment and gained relevant 'work-based experience'. SRA guidance also lists 53 examples of the many legal specialisms, from which the trainee must gain practical experience in at least three. The list includes: Corporate Finance; Employment; Family; Immigration Law; Libel and Defamation; International Law; Medical Negligence; Mergers and Acquisitions; Neighbour Disputes; Personal Injury; Planning Law; Taxation and Wills and Probate.

The Professional Skills Course (or PSC) is the final element of compulsory training which you will undergo before being formally admitted as a solicitor. You will take it at the end of your PRT. It builds on the foundations laid by the LPC and ensures that trainees receive formal instruction in matters better studied once the trainee has already had some exposure to practise. The PSC comprises three subject areas, namely: Financial and Business Skills; Advocacy and Communication Skills; Client Care and Professional Standards. There is a compulsory core element totalling 48 hours tuition in all three subjects and an elective element of 24 hours tuition followed by assessments. The compulsory element must normally be completed before the candidate can move on to the electives, which can be chosen from any of the following:

♦ Courses leading to the Higher Rights of Audience Qualification, or
♦ The Human Rights Act

There are no formal assessments for the PSC Electives.

On completion of the Advocacy and Communication Skills compulsory element, trainees should be competent to exercise those rights of audience which are routinely available to a solicitor in the civil and criminal courts. In particular trainees should be able to present a procedural application before a District Judge; use appropriate language; examine a witness and cross-examine an opposing witness; present arguments; open and close a case and deal with any ethical problems which might arise during the course of proceedings.

The compulsory element of Client Care and Professional Standards requires the trainee to identify and deal with their ethical responsibilities to: their clients; the court; other solicitors; other professionals; the SRA and other relevant bodies; their colleagues and themselves. This includes an ability to engage with clients in the taking of instructions, discussion of costs, handling client expectations, avoiding and handling complaints when they arise. It also involves professional standards, including: client confidentiality, identifying and handling conflicts of interest, the giving of professional undertakings and letters of engagement. Trainees must also be able to manage their own work and cases in a way which minimises risk.

As regards Accounting and Financial Issues, trainees should be aware of the potential need to involve other professionals (such as accountants or other financial specialists) when advising clients and also be able to identify the main investment products on the market and able to distinguish their main features and suitability for different types of client. Trainees must also understand what legislation is in place for regulating financial services; the rules to protect against money-laundering and how to be alert to the possibility of mortgage fraud.

Tips for Getting a Training Contract

◆ Try getting some paralegal work or other work-experience within a legal office. It will give you something to show on your CV and suggest that you already have insight into the work you can expect as a trainee .

◆ Take time to get your application form right. Make sure that there are no typos or other mistakes to create a bad impression.

◆ Learn as much as possible about the firm to which you

will be applying and tailor your application accordingly.

◆ Raise your profile through writing and blogging.

◆ Include in your CV any non-legal experience which shows business acumen or an understanding of customer service.

◆ Attend one of the twice yearly skills events offered by the Law Society's Junior Lawyers' Division, which will provide advice on how to stand-out and get that coveted training contract;

◆ Try to develop a personal connection with your preferred firm, so that they remember you when you apply for a training contract.

◆ Start early. Many firms look to fill training places two years in advance. It means that students should start applying towards the end of the second year of their law degree. What firms are looking for is an applicant's potential.

The Apprenticeship Route to Qualification

The apprenticeship route to solicitor qualification is the newest way for a school-leaver to get into the legal profession, without first having to go to university. Trailblazer Legal Apprenticeships are only part of wider Government initiative to create three million apprenticeships by 2020. To push the scheme forward the Government has imposed an Apprenticeship Levy on the 2% of employers who have an annual wage bill of more than £3M. That Levy amounts to 0.5% of the total wage bill less a fixed £15,000 allowance. The money raised is then used to fund apprenticeship training.

Firms paying into the scheme will then be given access to a digital account from which they can draw down funds for apprenticeship training according to an agreed Government formula. It means that there will now be a direct financial incentive for employers - both large and small - to offer apprenticeships. For the prospective trainee, getting an apprenticeship means no tuition fees and a paid opportunity to experience life in a legal office sooner rather than later. There are currently three legal apprenticeship schemes covering paralegals, chartered legal executives and solicitors.

So long as it meets the assessment criteria it is up to individual employers to structure the apprenticeship and set the entry requirements. The Solicitor Apprenticeship is expected to last five to six years, which may be reduced if the apprentice has previously completed the Paralegal or Chartered Legal Executive Apprenticeships. Recommended minimum entry requirements are five GCSEs (including maths and English – grade C and above) and three A Levels (minimum Grade C or equivalent). The apprenticeship is at Level 7, which means that it is at a degree level. The apprenticeship will include external examinations plus workplace assessment against an Apprenticeship Standard. The Part 1 Functioning Knowledge Tests combine an external examination coupled with a work-based assessment bench marked against the Apprenticeship Standard and Statement of Solicitor Competence and which is certified by the training provider or employer, both of which must be completed before the apprentice can sit Part 2.

The second Part 2 examination is the End-Point Assessment

comprising standardized practical legal examinations which are externally assessed. Once they have completed their work-based assessment and passed all modules in Parts 1 and 2 of the centralized assessment, an apprentice can apply to the SRA to be admitted as a solicitor, subject to satisfying the Character and Suitability Test.

Both Parts 1 and 2 are made up of separately assessed modules which can be sat separately, save that all of the Part 2 modules must be taken in the last six months of the apprenticeship. In Part 1 apprentices will be assessed on their ability to draw on and apply knowledge which is sufficient to enable them to practice effectively. The examinations themselves will comprise computer based objective tests requiring candidates to identify relevant legal principles and then apply them to factual issues which address a client's needs.

In Part 2, apprentices will be assessed in respect of their knowledge, skills and behaviours in the following areas namely: interviewing and advising; advocacy/oral presentation; negotiation; writing, drafting documents and correspondence; and legal research. The examination itself will utilise role plays and on-line case-studies. The assessment overall will be at graduate level but will not be graded. Currently law firms offering legal apprenticeships include: Addleshaw Goddard; Bond Dickinson; Browne Jacobson; Burges Salmon; Eversheds; Freeths; Freshfields; Gowling WLG; Kennedys; Mishcon de Reya; Pinsent Masons and many others, as well several local authorities and the BBC and ITV.

With more people wanting legal apprenticeships than there

are apprenticeships available, getting an apprenticeship is easily as competitive as getting a training contract. The difference is that your scramble for an apprenticeship begins as you are about to leave school, not after you have worked through a law degree and passed your LPC. So even if you don't get your legal apprenticeship, you still have time to qualify as a solicitor through one of the other routes described in this chapter.

The CILEX Route to Qualification

Even when entrance to the Solicitors' profession was graduate only, it was never completely graduate only as it has always been possible for someone firstly to qualify as a Legal Executive and then upgrade their qualification to that of solicitor. Lack of a university degree has never barred anyone from studying for the CILEX qualification and has never barred anyone from upgrading their CILEX qualification to that of solicitor. Around 25% of solicitors practicing today were former legal executives who had upgraded their qualifications.

The CILEX route to qualification is the longest route to becoming a solicitor as you first have to qualify as a Chartered Legal Executive. Only when you have done that can you convert your CILEX qualification to that of a solicitor. It is also the least-competitive as it does not involve scrambles either for apprenticeships or training contracts. It is also the most leisurely route to qualification, which might suit someone who is squeezing in their training between other family commitments or the demands of a full time job. There are fewer regulatory time-limits for passing examinations. You can do it in your own time.

Later we look in more detail at the process for qualifying as a Chartered Legal Executive. In the meantime we have jumped ahead to how that CILEX qualification can be upgraded to that of solicitor. Again there are several upgrading options which depend on the point from which you are starting.

If you have no prior legal training and do not want to study for a law degree, you can instead work through the CILEX Level 3 Professional Diploma in Law and Practice and the CILEX Level 6 Higher Diploma in Law and Practice. You will also need a minimum three years Qualifying Employment under the supervision of a solicitor, Chartered Legal Executive, Barrister or Licensed Conveyancer. The final two years must be served consecutively and the final year must be as a Graduate Member Grade of CILEX. You will also need to complete a portfolio of evidence showing that the work-based learning criteria have been met, as demonstrated by a logbook and portfolio covering 27 outcomes. This will substitute for the two year training contract which would otherwise be required. Having become a Chartered Legal Executive you can then embark on the SRA Legal Practice Course, so long as you have first contacted the SRA's Training and Education Department on 0370 606 2555 for confirmation that the route you intend to take will meet SRA requirements.

If you have already qualified as a Graduate Member of CILEX through the CILEX Level 6 Professional Higher Diploma in Law and Practice, your CILEX Level 6 subjects will count towards the SRA's Academic Stage of Training. It is then about passing CILEX Level 6 Single Subject Certificate exams in the remaining subjects from the SRA's core list, namely: tort; equity and trusts; contract; land law; public law; European law; and criminal law – plus one further law subject of your choice. Having satisfied the SRA's Academic Stage, you will then move on to the LPC. Again you will need to demonstrate three years Qualifying Employment.

If you are already a Graduate Member of CILEX after having obtained a law degree followed by the CILEX Graduate Fast Track Diploma, you have already satisfied the SRA's Academic Stage. And if you are already a Chartered Legal Executive through having completed your Qualifying Employment and also your LPC, you are now ready to upgrade your qualification to that of solicitor.

Proposals for Change

During 2015 through to 2017 the SRA have undertaken a consultation on changes to the solicitor qualification process to make it more consistent, transparent and to remove the main barrier to qualification: which is getting a two year training contract. The requirement for two year's workplace experience will remain but there will be greater flexibility as to how this can be obtained.

The changes are now confirmed by the SRA in an April 2017 announcement and are scheduled to take effect in September 2020. The key change is the replacement of the LPC by a new

Solicitor's Qualifying Examination (SQE). The main difference between the SQE and LPC is that with the SQE there will be an external centralised assessment delivered by a single provider. By contrast around 100 universities deliver the LPC, with pass rates varying from 50% to 100%. The proposed SQE will be split into Stage 1 and Stage 2.

Stage 1 will comprise six Functioning Legal Knowledge Assessments comprising: Principles of Professional Conduct; Public and Administrative Law and the Legal Systems of England and Wales; Dispute Resolution in Contract or Tort; Property Law and Practice; Commercial and Corporate Law and Practice; Wills and the Administration of Estates and Trusts; Criminal Law and Practice. In addition there will be a Practical Legal Skills Assessment relating to Legal Research and Writing.

Stage 2 will comprise five Practical Legal Skills Assessments in: Client Interviewing; Advocacy/Persuasive Oral Communication; Case and Matter Analysis; Legal Research and Written Advice; and Legal Drafting. Those five assessments must each be applied and passed in two practice contexts of the candidate's choice, making a total of ten assessments. The relevant practice contexts from which the candidate must choose are: Criminal Practice; Dispute Resolution; Property; Wills and the Administration of estates and Trusts; Commercial and Corporate Practice.

The SRA expects many candidates to take SQE Stage 1 before their work-based experience and Stage 2 at the end of their work experience. Stage 1 would be a computer based assessment using single best answer questions, extended matching questions and multiple choice questions.

As well as passing examinations the SRA will continue to require candidates to undertake a period of work-based learning but in a way which is more flexible than the current requirement for a formal two year training contract. Difficulties in securing training contracts in a competitive market will no longer be the barrier to qualification that it is at present. Instead, obtaining a formal training contract would be only one of a number of choices for demonstrating adequate workplace training. Suggested alternatives will include: working in a student law clinic; as an apprentice or paralegal or through a placement as part of a sandwich degree. Instead of assessing the quality of the work-experience, the SRA would test the candidate's competence via the SQE Stage 2. The expected period of workplace experience will remain at 24 months. The use of computer assessment at Stage 1 means that it is likely to be substantially cheaper for students than the current LPC. Students who are already part-way through the current process of qualification on the date the changes take effect will be able to choose whether to continue on that route or transfer to the new regime.

Chapter Thirteen

HOW TO QUALIFY AS A BARRISTER

The process of qualifying as a barrister is overseen by the Bar Standards Board, which represents the four Inns of Court. Like solicitors, the process of qualification is under review. Like solicitors, the process of qualification is competitive. So much so that the BSB, the Inns of Court and the Bar Council have issued a Health Warning to anyone thinking of training to be a barrister. The Health Warning states that the Bar can be an extremely rewarding career to someone: of high intellectual ability; who is highly articulate in written and spoken English; who can think and communicate under pressure; and has determination, stamina and who is emotionally robust. It then goes on to provide some statistics.

Out of approximately 1400 students who take the Bar Course every year, there will be a 'pupillage' for only around 433 (less than 30%). As will be seen later, a twelve-month pupillage is an essential requirement for anyone wanting to qualify as a barrister. A would-be barrister who fails to get a pupillage in the first year after completing the Bar Course normally has a further four years in which to seek pupillage. In some years more than 3,000 individuals may be applying for pupillages and some Chambers have more than one hundred applicants for each pupillage offered. But even getting a pupillage doesn't guarantee a career as a barrister. That depends on whether, as a qualified barrister, you can get a 'tenancy' at one of the Chambers. This is because there are normally fewer available tenancies than there are pupillages, which means that Chambers do not always offer tenancies to their own pupils. That said, we can now look at the process of barrister qualification. Like solicitor qualification, it is in three parts.

There is firstly the Academic Stage, comprising either a Qualifying Law Degree or – for non-law graduates – the one year post-graduate conversion course, namely the Common Professional Examination (or Graduate Diploma in Law). At this point, the Academic Stage for Barristers is exactly the same as that for Solicitors. It is at the next stage that the routes to qualification diverge. Instead of the LPC, would be barristers will study for the Bar Professional Training Course (BPTC).

This is a one year course if studied full time – or two years if studied part time. It is stated to be a programme of vocational training which equips prospective barristers with the essential knowledge, skills and attributes which are expected from any barrister starting out in practise. The course itself enables the development of barrister-skills through vocational training helping candidates to apply legal knowledge and develop an understanding of what it means to be a reflective and responsible practitioner with respect to professional ethics. But there are the following entry requirements for anyone wanting to embark on the course. These are:

- Completion of the Academic Stage (as above).
- Becoming a member of one of the four Inns of Court – namely, Lincoln's Inn, Inner and Middle Temples, and Grays Inn.
- Fluency in the English Language. On starting the course students must sign a statement that they are aware of the standard of English required and that they have met it. That standard is a minimum score of 7.5 in each section of the IELTS academic test or 73 in each part of the Pearson Test of English. If the course provider later considers that any aspect of the student's language is not to the required level, the student must within 28 days take a formal language test and provide a certificate that they have achieved the required scores.
- The student must take and pass a Bar Course Aptitude Test (BCAT), which is a test of critical thinking which does not require any legal knowledge. The outcome of the BCAT may give an intending student an indication of their likely success on the BPTC

The BCAT is a psychometric test which is taken online at a Pearson VUE Test Centre and comprises 60 multiple choice situations to be completed within a 55 minute slot and which requires candidates to exercise judgment when making assumptions. Whilst the formal assessment costs £150, there is practice assessment which anyone can access on-line without cost. That practice assessment is to the same format and standard as the actual assessment. Anyone completing the practice assessment will receive feedback via an on-line report which – on the basis of actual statistics – will indicate how well that person might be likely to score in an actual BCAT and in the BPTC itself. The limitations of BCAT – or indeed any IQ test – is that it can measure only a person's ability to pass an examination. Or to put it even more narrowly: their ability to pass a computerized, multi-choice IQ test. But critical thinking alone does not make someone into a great advocate.

When you are standing up in court, you are not feeding information into a computer. You are trying to convince real people. Just as important as critical thinking is an understanding of human nature. It is the ability to engage emotionally with your audience. It is your ability to create empathy. Your ability to win magistrates, judges or a jury over to your cause. George Carmen understood that. So did Denning. So did Churchill. So did Gandhi. So did Abraham Lincoln. So did Mandela. So did Martin Luther King. So did Shakespeare. How would they have scored on a critical thinking test? But perhaps BCAT is only one symptom of a creeping intellectualization of the law in which human concepts of right-and-wrong and fairness are pushed to the fringes. With Denning it was: justice first. Alas not anymore. How else would you explain the Supreme Court's majority decision in the 2015 case of Arnold v Britten, declaring the owners of individual holiday chalets liable for annual service charges rising from an estimated £2,500 per chalet in 1980 to £550,000 at lease-end? Or its 2016 decision in the Scottish Case of Campbell v Gordon, when it ruled - on a technicality - that an accident victim could not sue the director of an insolvent company who had neglected to put in place adequate employers' liability insurance which would have covered that injury. Even though that director had committed a criminal offence by failing to insure. There are human rights for some – but not for all.

Having undertaken the BCAT assessment and having fulfilled the other entry criteria, we now look at the Bar examination itself. The BPTC is made up of three main elements namely:

- Knowledge areas – comprising civil litigation and evidence; criminal litigation and sentencing; professional ethics;
- Skills areas – comprising advocacy; opinion writing; drafting; conference skills; resolution of disputes (both in and out of court);
- A range of specialist electives.

The assessments themselves comprise a mix of oral and closed-book examinations and are divided into:

- Formative (or informal) Assessments which are set by the course provider to enable students to practice and receive feedback in relation to advocacy, conferencing, opinion writing and drafting; and

- ◆ Summative (or formal) assessments in knowledge and practical subjects, which candidates will need to pass to get the BPTC.

There are also some subjects within the BPTC which are not formally assessed, namely: Legal Research Methods; Basic Management Skills; Pro Bono and Court Visits. There is also a 'Red Light Rule' which means that even if other parts of the examination are passed, a student will be failed if their legal or case analysis is so wrong that it would put a client's interests at risk or put the barrister at risk of liability for negligence or a disciplinary finding. A student may also be failed for a 'fatal flaw', which is a significant and grave error of law or procedure or which raises an ethics issue. Examples given of where the Red Light Rule would apply, include:

- ◆ Advice that a three-years-old personal injury claim is statute barred, without any consideration of other factors which might mean that the claim is still in time;
- ◆ A stale contract claim where counsel fails to advise that proceedings can no longer be brought because breach of contract had taken place more than six years earlier;
- ◆ Advice to a client to settle a civil claim when that client already has a water-tight defence, perhaps on grounds of limitation.

Pupillage

Pupillage is the final part of the qualification process to become a barrister. And if you thought getting a solicitor's training contract was competitive, imagine a situation where you are up against 99 other top class candidates for a single placement. Yes – with some chambers it is like that. It is why anyone seeking pupillage is advised to start early. Before even embarking on the BPTC. It means that there will often be a gap of more than a year between a student getting their pupillage and actually starting it.

Pupillage itself is the practical stage of barrister-training within a set of barristers' chambers (or other approved organization), which can be started up to five years after completing the BPTC. Most pupillages start in the September or October following acceptance.

Within the chambers, pupils will work under the supervision of other barristers. Each pupillage lasts for twelve months, which are split into a 'first six' and a 'second six'. The first six is a non-practising six months, during which pupils shadow their pupil supervisor, do legal research, draft opinions and other court documents, read their supervisor's paperwork and observe them in conferences or in court. During the second six, pupils undertake work themselves, but under supervision. If at the end of second six pupils have not yet been offered a tenancy they may do a third six either at the same or at a different chambers, in which they do their own work but are not yet tenants. Chambers offering pupillages are required to fund each pupillage with a minimum £12,000 award – split into £6,000 for each half.

To help would-be barristers find pupillages the Bar Council operates a Pupillage Gateway, which is an on-line application system for pupillage and onto which all vacancies are advertised for a minimum two weeks. The Bar Council also hosts a Pupillage Fair, providing an opportunity for students to meet chambers and other organizations offering information and opportunities.

Would-be barristers, who have not yet completed the BPTC are also encouraged to undertake 'mini-pupillages', which are short structured sessions of work experience to gain practical experience of different areas of law and life in chambers and other organizations and also undertaking as many public speaking opportunities as possible and volunteering with organizations which provide free or 'pro-bono' legal services.

As well as undertaking pupillage, students are also expected to participate in the social life and training courses provided by their Inn before being 'Called to the Bar'. They can also ask for a sponsor or mentor, being a practising barrister, who can provide practical advice and introduce them to life at the Bar. Students must also have completed twelve 'Qualifying Sessions' with their Inn, which might include residential training weekends, skills-based workshops or attending lectures, as well as formal dinners with barristers and judges. Being Called to the Bar takes the form of a ceremony in March, July, October or November.

Chapter Fourteen

HOW TO QUALIFY AS A CHARTERED LEGAL EXECUTIVE

Training to be a Chartered Legal Executive presents the most flexible and affordable mainstream entry into the legal profession. Unlike the barrister and solicitor examinations there are no minimum entry requirements for anyone wishing to embark on legal training. Although the Chartered Institute of Legal Executives (CILEX) assumes that candidates will have a minimum four GCSEs at Grade C or above, including English Language, that is not a mandatory requirement.

For anyone starting from ground-zero, CILEX recommends that candidates begin with the City & Guilds/CILEX Level 2 Certificate in Legal Studies before embarking on formal CILEX training. This introductory course is itself set equivalent to GCSE Level and comprises a compulsory core curriculum of: Legal Environment; Principles of Criminal Liability; Principles of Contract and Principles of Negligence. In addition to the four core subjects, the candidate must also choose an optional subject from a list comprising: Law in the Workplace; Civil Litigation; Family Law; Wills and Succession and Land and Conveyancing.

Each study-unit takes about 40 hours to complete, making 200 hours in total to achieve the Certificate. The Core Level 2 Subjects are assessed by an on-line multiple choice test, taken under the supervision of an employer or at an external City & Guilds approved venue.

CILEX training is also affordable as it can be studied part-time or by distance-learning through Cilex's own Law School. Like the driving test, there are no time limits for passing CILEX examinations. So if someone fails, first time round, they can re-sit, and re-sit again and again and again until they pass. And although qualification as a Chartered Legal Executive requires a sufficient period of workplace training, getting that training is not the competitive scramble it is for would-be solicitors or barristers.

Most aspiring Legal Executives begin with the CILEX Level 3 Professional Diploma in Law and Practice, which is made up of ten units and is designed to provide a good grounding in all core areas of the law and the flexibility to tailor the practice elements of the qualification to individual student requirements. The level 3 course comprises seven mandatory units, namely: Introduction to Law and Practice; Contract Law; Criminal Law; Land Law; Law of Tort; Client Care Skills and Legal Research Skills. For the remainder of the course, candidates must choose, either:

+ Two practice units from a list comprising: Civil Litigation; Conveyancing; Criminal Litigation; The Practice of Family Law; The Practice of Employment Law; Probate Practice; The Practice of Law for the Elderly Client; The Practice of Child Care Law or Residential and Commercial Leasehold Conveyancing. And one additional law unit from a list comprising: Employment Law; Family Law; Law of Wills and Succession.

+ Or any three practice units from the above list.

The only caveat as regards choice of practice units is that the chosen unit must also relate back to an equivalent law unit which is also being studied. So for example the 'conveyancing' practice unit will relate back to the compulsory 'Land Law' unit. In other words, practice units cannot be studied in isolation without equivalent knowledge of the law of the subject.

CILEX recommends that the Level 3 course is studied over a period of two years, by studying five units each year. Whilst units can be studied in any order, CILEX recommends that the first year studies relate to those units which can combine together to create one of the ten CILEX Certificates, so that at the end of that first year the candidate has achieved a recognized qualification. In the second year, candidates will need to cover off any of the mandatory subjects which they have not passed in the first year together with any optional subjects.

On successful completion of the Level 3 course, the student becomes an Associate Member of CILEX. The next step is the

Level 6 course to qualify as a Graduate Member of CILEX. As well as passing the Level 6 examination a period of qualifying employment is also required. To pass the Level 6 examination, a candidate must study six subjects in total comprising:

♦ One legal practice unit with its linked law unit;
♦ Two other law units of the candidate's choice;
♦ And the two mandatory professional skills courses, namely: Client Care Skills and Legal Research Skills.

The fourteen choices of Law Unit are: Company and Partnership; Contract; Criminal; Employment; Equity and Trusts; EU Law; Family; Immigration; Land Law; Landlord and Tenant; Public Law; Tort; Wills and Succession. The seven choices of Practice Unit are: Civil Litigation; Practice of Company and Partnership; Conveyancing; Criminal Litigation; Practice of Employment Law; Practice of Family Law; Probate Practice. As regards qualifying employment, what is required is work of a legal nature under the supervision of a solicitor, a Chartered Legal Executive, barrister or licensed conveyancer. The exact requirement is:

♦ Minimum three years' work-experience;
♦ Final two years to be served consecutively;
♦ Final year must be in Graduate Member Grade of CILEX;
♦ Completion of a portfolio of evidence which shows that the work-based learning criteria has been met, demonstrated by a logbook and portfolio covering 27 outcomes.

CILEX also offers concessions on the Level 3 examination for candidates who already have A Level Law or the Level 2 Qualification. But the biggest exemption is for candidates who already have a Qualifying Law Degree and who are therefore eligible for CILEX's Graduate Fast Track Diploma and who are not required to study any more law subjects to qualify as a Chartered Legal Executive. However they still have to study two Level 6 Practice Units as well as the Client Care Skills Unit. At least one of the chosen practice units must link back to a law unit studied as part of the degree. In that respect the Criminal Litigation; Civil Litigation and Conveyancing practice units all relate to a core law degree subject. Estimated study time for the Fast Track Diploma is nine to fifteen months. At the same time Fast Track students are recommended to take paralegal work which will count towards their period of qualifying employment.

The Chartered Legal Executive Apprenticeship is the newest route to CILEX qualification. It is a five year programme which comprises: all of the Level 3 and Level 6 Qualifications; qualifying employment and work-based learning requirements and completion of an extended case-study. However given the flexibility of the mainstream route to qualification it is difficult to see what advantages the apprenticeship route offers over other paralegal training.

At the end of the CILEX qualification process, candidates will have a stand-alone professional qualification which will enable them to earn a reasonable living within the legal market place. CILEX also offers Authorised Practitioner Status to

Chartered Legal Executives wanting to offer conveyancing, probate, litigation, advocacy and immigration services directly to the public. To obtain Authorised Status, practitioners must be able to demonstrate competence in their particular specialist area by showing:

- ◆ Either knowledge to honours degree standard in that subject area or work experience demonstrated through portfolios of five cases they have worked with;
- ◆ Experience of at least two years practise in that subject area demonstrated by producing three portfolios of cases;
- ◆ Skills in legal research, client care and practice in the relevant subject area, demonstrated by either a logbook and supporting evidence or skills courses completed;
- ◆ And for a CILEX regulated law firm, the practitioner must also show accounts and practice management knowledge, experience and skills.

Once issued with a CILEX Practising Certificate, practitioners can describe themselves as a CILEX Conveyancing, Litigation and Advocacy, Probate or Immigration Practitioner and provide the full range of services within those areas without supervision and apply to set up their own regulated businesses.

Whilst currently the CILEX qualification does not have quite the professional status of a solicitor qualification, it is something which can be upgraded at any time. But whether you choose to upgrade to solicitor or remain as a Chartered Legal Executive, your future career is essentially what you make it. If clients like you and the service you offer, they will pay for it.

Chapter Fifteen

BECOMING A LICENSED CONVEYENCER OR A PROBATE PRACTIONER

In many respects qualification as a licensed conveyancer is a professional cul-de-sac. The qualification itself came about as a result of the conveyancing wars of the early 1980s, when Thatcher's Conservative Government legislated to break the solicitors' monopoly on conveyancing work by creating a new profession with its own qualification structure and professional standards. It was the Administration of Justice Act 1985 which paved the way for the new profession and set out the framework for qualification and its future regulation by a newly established Council for Licensed Conveyancers (CLC). Although originally only for conveyancers, the CLC has now offered the option for qualification as a Licensed Probate Practitioner and also has its sights on the provision of litigation and advocacy services.

Until 2014 Licensed Conveyancers were the only people, other than solicitors, who could set up their own business and compete head-to-head in the legal market place. But they are limited to two narrow spheres of work: conveyancing and probate. What changed in 2014 is that CILEX Authorised Practitioners can now set up business and do the same. But the CLC qualification lacks the fluidity of CILEX in that there is no mainstream process for upgrading a Licensed Conveyancer qualification to that of a solicitor. Nevertheless the CLC qualification still provides a comparatively low cost alternative to professional qualification and is also one in which candidates are not competing with each other for training places. The CLC's qualification process is currently administered by the Scottish Qualifications Authority (SQA).

To qualify as a 'CLC Lawyer' a candidate must *either*:

♦ Complete the CLC's Level 4 Diploma in Conveyancing Law and Practice followed by the Level 6 Diploma; or

♦ Complete the Level 4 Diploma in Probate Law and Practice followed by the Level 6 Diploma.

There are no minimum entry requirements before embarking on training process, although it is suggested that the Level 2 English and Mathematics qualifications may be helpful. There is also no requirement for anyone to be in a legal services job in order to study for a Diploma. However anyone applying for a Conveyancing or Probate Licence must complete a Statement of Practical Experience confirming that they have been in full or part-time paid, or voluntary, employment assisting in the provision of conveyancing or probate services for at least 1,200 chargeable hours; based on 25 supervised hours a week for 48 weeks and certified by an 'Authorised Person' (being a licensed conveyancer, solicitor or Fellow of CILEX who is licensed to offer conveyancing or probate services directly to the public).

The Level 4 Diploma in Conveyancing Law aims to provide students with a theoretical and basic practical understanding of:

- The legislative and court system in England and Wales;
- The principles underpinning the creating of a binding contract and its performance;
- The modern English land law system within an historical context;
- The law and procedures relating to a standard conveyancing transaction;
- Mortgages and standard lender requirements;
- The different ways in which property can be owned;
- NHBC guarantees;
- Powers of Attorney, Court of Protection and associated issues;
- An understanding of leases and tenancies and how they are created;
- Associated lease-issues, including assignment, Licences to Assign, assignments and freehold enfranchisements;
- The system for accounting for monies held on behalf of clients and the regulatory framework which governs such

accounting as well as anti-money laundering legislation.

The whole course is estimated to require a total of 250 guided learning hours, which does not of course include additional preparation, reading-up and revision time. The English Legal System assessment is based on short answer questions and mini case-studies. The law of Contract is essay based and/or short answer restricted response questions. Land Law is assessed on the basis of case-studies. Accounting procedures is based on short answer or multiple choice questions and the recording of transactions using a double-entry system as well as production of a client-invoice for a conveyancing transaction and the preparation of a financial statement.

The Level 6 Conveyancing Diploma is intended to equip the student with the required theoretical knowledge of:

◆ Leasehold covenants and obligations and available options in the event of default;

◆ The different types of residential tenancies and how they are affected by the Rent Act 1977 and the Housing Act 1988.

◆ The difference between residential, commercial and agricultural leases and which statutes apply in each case.

◆ Individual and collective freehold enfranchisement and a residential leaseholders' collective right of first refusal when a freehold is about to be sold;

◆ The areas of law which impact on a land sale and purchase transaction;

◆ All the stages of a residential sale and purchase in

registered and unregistered land; freehold and leasehold transactions from initial instructions until after completion including CLC professional conduct rules;

* The requirements of mortgage lenders and the need to consider money laundering issues;

* The remedies for breach of a sale contract and how they should be applied;

* Client Account entries and the application of the CLC Code;

* Preparing a completion statement;

* The system of Practice Accounting Records, including office account entries and trial balance;

* The banking system and Bank reconciliation statements;

* Year-end accounts including accounting concept, adjustments and analysis and cash flow forecasting.

The Level 6 examination requires an estimated 281 guided learning hours and assessment is mainly based on candidate responses to case-study scenarios. The exception is the accounting aspects, in which candidates will be assessed on their recording of financial transactions by requiring to produce, from a Trial Balance, a Profit and Loss Account, Balance Sheet, an appropriation account, bank reconciliation statement and a cashflow statement.

The Level 4 Diploma in Probate Law and Practice contains similar content as its conveyancing equivalent but with emphasis on the law and procedures relating to the formation of wills and associated testamentary documents; the administration, winding up and distribution of a deceased person's estate and accounting procedures for probate transactions. The Level 6 Diploma in Probate Law and Practice aims to equip the student with the required theoretical knowledge as regards:

- Clients presenting themselves for advice on a will or codicil and the duty of care owed to them;
- The legal requirements for making a will in terms of testamentary capacity and formalities of execution;
- The types of bequests and legacies typically found in a will;
- The application of CLC Professional Conduct and Guidance Rules and principles to will-making clients and personal representatives;
- The requirements of registering a death and measures needed to protect a personal representative;
- The Non-Contentious Probate Rules insofar as they apply to Limited Grants and applications to the Probate Registry for searches, caveats, citations and directions;
- Dealing with problems and issues arising during the administration of an estate;
- The circumstances when succession takes place independently of a will or rules of succession;
- Potential claims for reasonable provision under the Inheritance (Provision for Families and Dependents) Act 1975;
- The rules relating to an insolvent estate;
- Client Account entries and the application of the CLC Accounts Code;

◆ The preparation of completion statements;

◆ The system of Practise Accounting Records, including office account entries, the trial balance;

◆ The banking system and Bank reconciliation statements;

◆ Year-end accounts including account concepts, adjustments and analysis and cash flow forecasting;

◆ The taxation implications of an estate with particular reference to Income Tax, Inheritance Tax and Capital Gains Tax.

The Level 6 Probate Diploma requires an estimated 211 Guided Learning Hours plus additional learning time. The Level 6 Assessment is largely case-study based.

The CLC provides exemptions for conveyancing practitioners wishing to cross-over to probate and vice-versa. Existing conveyancing practitioners wishing to apply for a Probate Licence are exempted the Level 4 Diploma in Probate Law and Practice but must complete two Level 6 Units, namely: Unit 1 (Wills, Succession and Grants of Representation) and Unit 2 (Administration of Estates). Existing Licensed Probate Practitioners wishing to apply for a Conveyancing Licence are exempted the Level 4 Conveyancing Diploma but must complete two Level 6 Units, namely: Unit 1 (Landlord and Tenant) and Unit 2 (Conveyancing Law and Practice). Existing solicitors or FCILEX wishing to apply for a Conveyancing or Probate Licence are automatically exempt from the Level 4 Diploma and may also qualify for exemption from some Level 6 Units. However all solicitors and FCILEX wishing to apply for a CLC Licence must as a minimum complete Unit 3 of the level 6 Diploma (Managing Client and Office Accounts – Conveyancing or Probate).

Chapter Sixteen

BECOMING A PARALEGAL, LEGAL SECRETARY OR BARRISTER'S CLERK

At one time paralegals were known as solicitors-clerks. They undertook administrative tasks, such as preparing standard-form documents or attending court-offices to issue proceedings. By undertaking such work, they freed up the solicitor's time to deal with more complex matters. In some public sector organisations paralegals are termed 'Legal Assistants'. But elsewhere the phrase 'paralegal' is used to describe anyone undertaking legal work within a law firm who does not have a recognized legal qualification, such a solicitor, barrister, chartered legal executive or licensed conveyancer. But that doesn't necessarily mean that they are without legal qualifications.

Many paralegals are law graduates whom, for whatever reason, do not have a formal training contract. Others may be foreign qualified lawyers who have yet to convert their qualification to something which is professionally recognised in England and Wales. There will also be paralegals fresh out of school or whose only qualification is the on-the-job experience they have picked up whilst in post. Whilst there is no formal regulatory process to become a paralegal, there is the National Association of Licensed Paralegals, which assists in career development and provides an optional legal qualification structure at three levels (Level 3, Level 4 and Level 7) which lends itself to distance learning. The organisation also maintains a Professional Paralegal Register. However for many people, working as a paralegal is a stop-gap pending formal training as a solicitor, chartered legal executive or licensed conveyancer. As paralegals can never offer legal services on their own account, they will always need to work under supervision and someone more formally qualified will need to take responsibility for their work.

A legal secretary has always been more than someone who can type accurately and at speed. Yes – accuracy will always be critical. Typing mistakes in a legal document can – at best – give clients an impression of sloppiness and – at worst – lead to an expensive negligence claim against a firm. A good team of legal secretaries is also key to the efficient running of any firm in a competitive market place. Without good administrative support, lawyers would have to carry out routine administrative tasks themselves, which would in turn get in the way of their more important task of fee-earning, without which the entire edifice would collapse. It is why a good legal secretary is worth a premium.

Whilst top legal secretaries can type at speeds approaching 120 words-per-minute, the amount of volume typing which legal secretaries are now required to produce has reduced because of the advent of case-management systems and computer packages which has enabled much standard form correspondence and documentation to self-generate from data which has been inputted. An example of such a computer package is 'Practical Law', which contains standard-form documentation for most lawyer-work. It follows that what is now more important for a legal secretary is their ability to use those case management systems. As well as typing and document preparation, much of a legal secretary's work now includes such things as processing conveyancing searches, downloading Land Registry title information and any other administrative tasks which are delegated to them. And there is something else. The legal secretary is often the interface between the lawyer and the outside world. Whilst the lawyer is engaged in meetings, client-interviews or court hearings, it is the secretary who will be first point of contact – or the public face of the firm – for any client, prospective client or anyone needing to do business with the lawyer.

Legal Secretaries are represented by the Institute of Legal Secretaries and PAs, which was formed in 1990 to promote the excellence and professional recognition of legal secretaries and personal assistants and which includes a range of qualifications to enable secretaries to gain the legal knowledge and practical skills they need to make the most of their careers. These include the Legal Secretaries Diploma Course, which covers different areas of the law and the practical tasks involved with legal secretary work, such as the production of legal documents and forms and professional correspondence, and which includes the option to go on a tour of the Royal Courts of Justice. The ILSP also offers an online typing skills course to help would-be legal secretaries get the recommended minimum 50 words-per-minute which they will need to work efficiently in a legal office. The on-line course is designed to teach touch-typing, increase typing speed and improve accuracy – with beginner, intermediate, advanced and speciality lessons. Being a legal secretary is also never a one-stop shop. Many legal secretaries utilise the legal knowledge and skills which they acquire from their day-to-day work to undertake more formalized legal training to qualify as chartered legal executives or solicitors

Whilst formal legal training is not a mandatory requirement for a barrister's clerk, they need to know enough about the law and procedures to do their job. It is why the Institute of Barristers' Clerks in conjunction with Central Law Training have produced a four-unit qualification covering the following subjects:

- Barristers' Clerks – Their Work in Context;
- Understanding the English Legal System;
- Communication Skills;
- Practical Learning.

The course is open to barristers' clerks with up to three years chambers experience and the bulk of the training takes place on-line over twelve months. However there is a half day face-to-face introduction at the start of the course and assessments at the end of each Unit.

Chapter Seventeen

YOUR FIRST LEGAL JOB

Let's assume that you have completed your training or pupillage and that you are now a fully fledged solicitor, licensed conveyancer, chartered legal executive or barrister. Where do you go from here?

Many newly qualified lawyers will want to stay - at least for the time being - with the firm or chambers in which they undertook their training. But that depends on two things. Do you want to stay with them? But more importantly. Do they want to stay with you? No - don't take it personally. The issue may be whether there is a vacancy for you to move into. In many cases the answer will be 'no'. Even if your employer is gracious enough to keep you on for the time being in your existing trainee role and salary - that is only a temporary stop-gap until you can find another job. So how do you go about finding another job?

It's the same problem you had getting your apprenticeship, training contract or pupillage. It's about putting together a

CV containing your academic qualifications, job history and experience. But it is the 'experience' which will always be the difficult one. It is why, as a newly qualified practitioner, prospective employers will be more interested in your potential to advance the interests of the firm. Yes - you would have been exposed to different areas of law and practice during your traineeship. But it was always with someone else looking over your shoulder to make sure that you are doing things correctly. But now you will have to take charge of that responsibility for yourself.

Getting your first qualified job is also the point at which you need to think about the type of organisation for which you want to work and the specialist areas of law within which you wish to develop your future career. And it is specialisation which is the key to a successful legal career. It is about finding something in which your expertise can shine through. As part of your training you would have already chosen options as regards the courses you studied to obtain your qualification. Now is the time to reflect on those choices - as the further down the career path you progress, the harder it is to change track. In choosing a specialisation, there are several factors which you need to consider:

◆ Is it something about which you are passionate? If reading through a sixty page lease makes you yawn, don't become a conveyancer. If you've no patience listening to the whinging of a divorcing spouse, then matrimonial law perhaps isn't for you. Would you like to spend long nights as a police station duty solicitor? No? Then don't make a career in the criminal law.

• Is it marketable? Becoming a residential conveyancer might not be the highest paid branch of the law. But there is a wide market for residential conveyancers. Millions of people buy and sell properties every year. Each one will require the services of a conveyancer. The only problem with the conveyancing market is that it fluctuates with the property market. When that property market is buoyant, conveyancers are in demand. When the market is flat, conveyancers are the first to be laid off. Contrast that with the position of a planning lawyer. Most planning lawyers work for local authorities and a few big solicitor firms who carry out work for local authorities or developers. But outside those restricted markets there is little demand for planning lawyers. Look at lawyer advertisements to get an idea what specialisms are most in demand and where.

• How much does it pay? You might enjoy suing debtors in the small claims court. Someone's got to do it. But that type of work is never going to make you rich. And it might not even make you an attractive prospect for employers. Again, for an idea as to what specialisations are most sought after and pay the most, look at lawyer advertisements. You will find them in the Law Society Gazette; CILEX Journal; The Lawyer Magazine and other journals. You will also find them on line. Which are the particular specialisations which are most sought after and are paying a premium? Thirty years ago it was commercial property lawyers and company lawyers who got the gold plated salaries. Today the market may be different. But it is dangerous to rely on a single specialisation: particularly at the beginning of a legal career. It is why your aim should be to build up a raft of compatible specialisations so that you can move with the market. If your specialisation is in planning law, think of another specialisation which would go with it. Conveyancing provides an example, as both are related to land and its development.

As regards getting your first lawyer-job, look at the advertisements appearing in Law Society Gazette and other legal journals. Look at their on-line pages and you will see thousands more. You will also discover that although styles may differ, most lawyer-advertisements follow a similar format as regards the information they provide to prospective candidates. For example the information provided by a typical lawyer advertisement might be distilled down as follows:

- Who is required? A Residential Conveyancer;
- Who for? A large provincial firm;
- What experience is required? Up to 2 years PQE
- What is on offer? An attractive remuneration package for the right candidate.
- Details on how to apply.

PQE refers to post-qualification experience. It means that this particular advertiser might consider someone who is newly qualified. In other words: you. As well as browsing advertisements and registering for on-line job alerts, the other ways to find legal jobs is through legal recruitment agencies such as Badenoch and Clark or Sellick Partnership – and of course networking.

A legal recruitment agency will help you prepare a professional CV and get you interviews. Another advantage of going through an agency is that they know the market and can advise you what remuneration package you should be seeking. If you are successful at interview it is the agency which will then act as an intermediary when negotiating your starting salary. If they succeed in placing you in a job, they will earn a commission geared to your starting salary, so it is in their interest to negotiate as high as the job is worth. But that commission will be paid by your employer, not you. Employers like employment agencies because they take the legwork out of recruitment. The agency will vet each prospective applicant to ensure compliance with employment regulations and to ensure that their qualifications, skills and experience sufficiently meets the 'person specification' provided by their client. Instead of ploughing through dozens of average CVs, it is the agency who will do that and present the employer with the best. There are of course other ways to find that crucial first job, through networking and getting the word out.

As a newly qualified lawyer, all you have to offer are your qualifications, that little bit of supervised experience which you obtained through your training contract and - most importantly - your enthusiasm. You have also found out – from your internet research – everything that you need to know about the firm or organization to which you are applying. It is all then down to how you perform in interview. If you are unsuccessful after your first few attempts, try to find out where you are going wrong and try to rectify it next time round. Always ask the firm or agency for feedback. Now let's suppose that you have succeeded in getting your first legal job. It is what happens in the first few years of that first job which can determine what will happen during the rest of your legal career. Remember that qualification is only the gateway to a legal career. That career itself is what you make it.

Learning to be a lawyer does not end with the expiry of your training contract. That is only the start of a process. Your objective during those crucial first few years should be about making yourself marketable as someone who knows their job, and who can be trusted to get things done, please clients and meet demanding financial targets as regards fees earned. Think of the law as a trade – or as a package of trades - in which knowhow is key.

No matter how glowing your academic achievements, it takes more than book-learning and examinations to master a trade. You need to get a 'feel' for the job. The same is true of the law. You may have begun to get some of that 'feel' during your on-the-job training. But that learning cannot stop at the end of your training contract. It has to continue post-qualification and throughout your career.

You may have already noticed that many lawyer-advertisements are looking for someone with around five years post qualification experience. In other words, the advertiser is saying that they want a candidate with sufficient experience to do the job but not someone who is too set in their ways, which might be the case with a longer-qualified candidate. There is also the assumption that a good solicitor with more than five years PQE would already be on their way to partnership or directorship within their existing firm. So why would they be looking round for another job?

The moment you start your first job you are an unknown quantity. All your employer and colleagues know about you is what is contained in your CV and the impression which you gave at interview. Apart from that, a couple of references, and perhaps a good word from your recruitment consultant, that is all they have to go on. The same is true of the existing clients of the firm with whom you will be dealing.

Those clients will have already had a good rapport with your predecessor, otherwise they would not still be clients. Now that person has gone and they have to deal instead with you. They say that you only have 90 seconds to make a good first impression. That may be true at interview and when you meet clients and colleagues for the first time. But the bottom line is that you have about four months from starting your new job to establish your credentials. With most new jobs comes a honeymoon period whilst employer and colleagues give you a month to settle in. Those weeks will soon pass Then comes the tough part as you try to 'crack' the job.

'Cracking' the job means establishing yourself as someone in whom clients and colleagues can place complete confidence. It means demonstrating that you are someone who knows the job, works efficiently, meets client and colleague expectations, gets results, and achieves monthly targets. In other words you are a 'safe pair of hands.' In those crucial few months you also hope that nothing seriously goes wrong which will undermine that confidence – like losing a client. Yes – there will always be hiccups. But if your reputation is damaged, it can be impossible to climb back.

You will know the exact moment when you have won over an existing client because they will make you their first point of contact instead of your boss. They will choose to telephone you when they want to 'sound out' your opinion on something or if they simply want someone in whom to confide. Nothing wrong with that so long as you do not breach internal protocols or undermine colleagues. Remembering also to make a note of any advice given. It's all about establishing relationships.

The Eureka moment will always result from a specific event which has impressed your client. It might be a piece of work which you have turned around quickly. It might be a result which you have achieved against difficult odds. It might be some practical advice which has solved a knotty problem for them. When a client asks you for advice, they don't just want a statement of the law. They can look that up for themselves. They want you to look at the matter from their point of view, advise them of their options and make a recommendation. What would you do in their situation? It is also about understanding the pressures which your client is under.

A private client may be concerned with the cost of your service. But for a busy commercial client, it is all about convenience. They want a lawyer who can take the burden from their shoulders, even if they have to pay more for it. If they are happy with your service they won't usually quibble the cost, provided that they can budget for it.

Just as important is the relationship which you establish with your colleagues. It is about 'showing willing'. It is about being someone who can take on new work and challenges without issue. It is about a willingness to volunteer – or to step into the breech to finish off an urgent piece of work for another fee-earner. It is about adopting the firm's dress-codes, conventions and ways of working. It is about being self-sufficient whilst at the same time making best use of available resources to help you work efficiently. It is about respecting the pressures which your colleagues are under.

Accumulating post qualification experience is about building up knowhow from your work, colleagues and surroundings. It is about taking a genuine interest in your colleagues and their work. Except when they are rushed off their feet (which you will find is most of the time), you will find that most colleagues are quite happy to talk about their work and provide practical tips on how you can carry out your own work better or more efficiently. They may even ask you for your opinion on matters related to their work. Books and courses can teach you about the law and process. Everything else has to be learned on-the-job. Something which can only be learned through practice is the dictation of volume correspondence and standard form documentation using an audio-system. Your ability to dictate work is key to being able to work at speed. That is of course assuming that you have an audio-secretary to dictate to.

Just as important as being able to do the work is your ability to get the work in the face of competition from other lawyers and law firms who are competing for the same work and client-base. Getting that work will not be so much of a problem if you are working for a large or medium size firm with an existing client base and a structured marketing strategy. But you are still up against the gravitational 'pull' which the largest and most successful UK law firms have already acquired when it comes to drawing in quality work. If you are going out for your weekly shop, you are more likely to go to Tesco, Sainsbury or Asda than the small corner supermarket. They are the market leaders when it comes to grocery shopping. Likewise if you need something electrical, Currys is likely to be amongst your first ports of call. For DIY it is B&Q or Homebase. For car-parts it is Halfords. It means that smaller independent retailers have to work that much harder to win their custom. It is the same with the law.

This doesn't mean such brand-leaders can take their clients and their incoming work for granted. It takes time and effort to establish a brand and any reputation is only as good as the lawyers who work for the organization – plus a strong enough marketing budget. Even then, there is nothing to stop an established client taking away their work overnight and moving it to another firm if they think they can get a better deal. But so long as those players continue to meet client expectations, their future is secure. Things are different for smaller firms: even those which have been around for centuries.

There is always leakage around an existing client-base. Clients die. Clients move away. Someone's death or house-move may generate some last-minute work for the firm. And then the client is gone. It means that new clients and work streams have to be found to top up the tank. Working in such a firm means that you will also need to play your part in bringing new work and clients to the firm as well as holding on to the existing client-base.

Whilst there is no substitute for a job-well-done, getting new work means drawing on all of your people and communication skills. It is about getting the word out that you are in business. It is about investing your own time to get out and meet people. But not in a high pressure way. Customers want to buy. They don't want to be sold-to. It also means building a platform for yourself. But there is more to it than just spreading the word.

Why should a prospective client instruct you – and not that other lawyer who works down the road? For some private clients it is purely about price – particularly when it comes to residential conveyancing. For other clients it is quality of service. Or perhaps they are seeking some specific expertise which you have but which most other lawyers don't. What is your unique selling point?

Your ability to keep existing clients and win new clients also has its own value in building a legal career. It is your 'goodwill'. If in the future you are intending to move to another firm, you are likely to be asked about your 'client following'. These are clients with whom you are so well established that they will take their work to your new firm. Having an established 'client following' is even more important if in the future you may be intending to set up in business on your own account. Finally it is the first few years in your first job that you will develop your specialisations. It is those specialisations and the reputation which you can establish with them which will become your magnet for attracting work and new clients. One way to draw attention to your expertise – apart from a job well done – is to write for your firm's newsletter (if it has one) or to offer articles to the local press and trade-journals operating in the areas in which you wish to practise. Remember that you are not writing to impress other lawyers. Your contributions are your point of contact with the people and trades that, at some time in the future, might want to use your service. And it is not just about writing. Also look for opportunities to give – or participate in – stand-out PowerPoint presentations. Building a professional reputation is hard work. Don't underestimate it.

So far we have looked only at private practice: which is by far the biggest area of legal-employment. All in all 75% of lawyers work in practise. But there are other in-house options. We have already seen that around 25% of lawyers work in-house. Let's look again at those options.

Most of the UK's largest companies have in-house legal teams of sorts. But generally their roles are not to undertake all of the legal work generated by their companies. The bulk of that work will still be farmed out to private solicitors. The role of the company-solicitor is to provide the interface between the Board of Directors and those outside firms. It may also be the Head of Corporate Counsel who is most influential in selecting those outside-firms, negotiating the terms of business and in managing the work from the client-side. And in signing off those solicitor-invoices. But there will still be some strategic or corporate work which the in-house lawyer carries out directly. This will include providing day-to-day advice and recommendations to directors or other senior officers and – for the most senior lawyers – attending company board meetings. The Head of Corporate Counsel may also be one of the public faces of a large company and may double up in other corporate roles, such as Company Secretary. It follows that key specialisations for a senior company lawyer is an expert knowledge of Company Law, Intellectual property law and the ability to negotiate their way around a commercial contract. They also need a thorough understanding of the industry within which they are working. Company lawyers are represented by the Law Society's Commerce and Industry Group. Lawyers working for housing associations and the voluntary sectors will have a similar 'interface' role.

With local government and other public sector organisations the situation is generally different in that the bulk of the work generated is dealt with 'in house' by the organisation's own lawyers. Legal work will only be outsourced to private firms when there is specific reason to do so. Such outsourcings may arise where some specific legal expertise is required which does not exist within the in-house team or where the sudden volume of work required for the timely delivery of a major project is, in terms of resource, beyond the capacity of the in-house team. It follows that – in terms of head-count – a local authority legal department will be several times bigger than a comparable company legal-team because it is trying to do everything. The reason for this is always 'cost'. The cost of an in-house lawyer's time is around £90 per hour. Compare this with £190 for an external lawyer's time. That £190 may itself be lower than what the private firm might charge other clients who do not have the same negotiating power. But that is the marketplace. And it is still twice the cost of using the organisation's own lawyers.

With local authorities – as with private non-corporate clients – cost is a driving factor. It is why many local authorities have combined together to bulk-negotiate external lawyer panels in which private firms have had to bid against each other for the right to be included on those panels. Because of European free-trade rules, public sector organisations do not have the same freedoms to pick and choose external lawyers in quite the same way as a private company. They have to follow due process. It is the same need to drive down costs which has led many local authority legal departments to merge together to form vast 'shared service organisations', each serving several public sector clients. HB Public Law and the South London Legal Partnership, each serve multiple local authorities. Working for a shared-service organization will in some respects mirror private practice in that you work for several clients and your time is charged out. But you are still constrained by the bureaucratic structures of a large public sector organization.

Whilst many general conveyancers and litigators work within local government, there are also other specialisations for which it is the key market. These include: town and country planning; child care; environmental law; housing and public law. Local government also provides an alternative career path for lawyers – of which the Head of Legal Services – or even Chief Executive – provides the pinnacle. Much of local government law is also administrative and includes attending committees to provide advice as well as guidance to elected members on points-of-order or other constitutional issues. The downside of working in local government is that it can be a one way street. Stay there too long and it may be difficult to work anywhere else. Not a problem if your ambition is to be Chief Executive.

The recruitment process for a public sector job is also longer, more structured and exhausting than for recruitment elsewhere. There are strict procedures to be followed to ensure absolute fairness in the treatment of candidates. Shortlisting candidates for interview involves scoring written job-applications against the skills and experience of an ideal candidate (or person specification). Each of candidates who are invited to interview are then asked exactly the same cryptic interview-questions and their responses scored against a set of model answers. In short it is a game played by each candidate against the interviewers and the other candidates. The one who scores the most points is the one who 'wins' the job – even if that person is not the interviewers' preferred choice. If you like crosswords - you will also be good at public sector interviews.

Chapter Eighteen

CAREER NEXT STEPS

You've held down your first job as a newly-qualified lawyer and perhaps have already moved between several firms. You are confident in your work and are building your reputation as someone who can be trusted to get results. Clients and prospective clients are already coming to you as their preferred point of contact. In short you are building a following. So what are you going to do next?

You may already see prospects for promotion within the firm in which you are already working. Otherwise it is about searching the market. Your billings and your following are your selling points. That is what you will bring to your new employer. A traditional career path for a solicitor be in private practice might be:

◆ Associate Solicitor. In other words you are someone who is employed by but as yet does not hold any stake in the firm. Yes- you may be mentioned on the notepaper. But maybe not.

Even though you will be responsible for your own workload, you will still be working under the supervision of a partner.

- ◆ Salaried Partner. This is about recognition. You are still a salaried employee of the firm but have earned the right to have your name printed on the notepaper. But you are still not fully a stakeholder in the firm. Your remuneration package may include bonuses but not a share of the firm's profits. However as salaried partner your personal assets may still be at risk if the firm goes down and the assets of the equity partners are insufficient to cover the whole of the firm's liabilities.

- ◆ Equity Partner. Now you are really part of the firm and have a direct financial stake in its fortunes. You are no longer employed but are now have a self-employed status. You may still get a salary but will also now have the right to share in the profits of the firm – or contribute towards its losses. The person at the top is the 'Senior Partner'.

Until recent years all solicitors' firms were set up as partnerships or as sole-practitioners. It meant that if something went wrong , it was the partners' homes and other personal assets which were at risk. In practice much of that risk would be covered off by the firm's professional indemnity insurance. But insurance cannot cover everything. A commercial loss may be so large that it extends beyond the available insurance cover. Or that cover may have been invalidated for other reasons. It is for that reason that, following changes in SRA rules, many firms have now re-established themselves as limited companies or limited liability partnerships. It means that the partners' personal liabilities for the firms losses are limited to their actual investment in the company or LLP. Now for 'Associate Solicitor' read 'Associate Director'. For 'Partner' read 'Director'. For 'Senior Partner' read 'Managing Director'. However adequate professional indemnity insurance is still a mandatory SRA requirement for law firm: whether it is a sole practitioner; traditional partnership; limited liability partnership or company. Without such insurance cover, anyone suing the firm for professional negligence could be left without financial redress if the company or LLP simply folds and there are no assets against which to attach. There are also many reasons why it is considered better to work with other solicitors than alone. And in this respect 'partnership' is also taken to include LLPs and companies.

Key to any successful conveyancing practice is a firm's appointment to the conveyancing panels of mainstream mortgage lenders. If the firm is not on the conveyancing panel, then it can't act for the relevant bank or building society in any conveyancing transaction. The mortgage lender will instead insist on instructing its own panel firm to act for it in the relevant house purchase, even if the buyers have chosen another firm to act for them. What this means is that the buyer will have to pay two sets of legal fees: their own and the mortgage lender's. Either that or the buyer's take their work away and instruct another firm which is on the lender's panel. Getting professional indemnity insurance and at an affordable cost can also be a problem for sole practitioners. Desperation for sufficient incoming work to pay the bills also makes some sole-practitioners a target for conveyancing-fraudsters.

Whilst every mortgage lender has its own criteria for deciding who will be on its conveyancing panel, it is fair to say that sole practitioners will not be top of the list. Lenders prefer medium to larger firms because there are more checks and balances. An established partnership also guarantees continuity. If one solicitor is indisposed, there are always others who can pick up the reins. It is also the sole practitioners and the smallest partnerships who statistically have more than their share of SRA interventions and disciplinary problems. And whilst there are no doubt some excellent sole practitioners, there is always the suspicion that some solicitors are sole practitioners because there is no-one else willing to work with them. But for lawyers brave enough to do so, setting up their own firm remains the next option for career progression. Up to 1000 new solicitor firms are formed each year.

Not all of these new firms are sole-practitioners. Some are partnerships. In some cases the new firms are fragmentations of existing firms. But the setting up process is the same. As regards formality, the starting point is the SRA's Firm Authorisation Application Form (FA1) setting details of what is proposed in relation to the new firm and how the business will be run. Applicants must also complete Form FA2 providing details about key personnel within the firm. Any solicitors firm must have amongst its personal someone who is 'Qualified to Supervise' This means that they must have worked as a solicitor for at least 36 months within the previous ten years and must have also undertaken a twelve hour management skills training course. There is also a chunky application fee. Setting up a new firm also requires significant investment and risk.

Even if you are intending to work from home and be your own secretary, receptionist, book-keeper and office-junior, you still have to meet the cost of your professional indemnity insurance – if you can get it. For partnerships, the SRA require a minimum level of cover of £3,000,000 for a single claim. To assist sole practitioners the minimum cover level is reduced to £2,000,000. It sounds a lot until you remember that the average London house-price in London tops £500,000.

Even for established firms the cost of professional indemnity insurance amounts to an estimated 2% to 5% of fee income, making it the largest single overhead after payment of salaries and office-accommodation costs. So if you are launching into setting up your own law-firm you need make pretty sure that you are going to have enough incoming quality work both to meet your overheads and provide you with a decent living. If you don't you may end up working twelve hour days earning money to put in someone else's pocket. So who are all these new clients who are going to be knocking on your door?

Perhaps the lawyers who are best placed to set up on their account are those with a specific niche specialisation within which no-one else can compete. Are you the best trade-marks lawyer in town? Think of Nick Freeman, who built his reputation on motoring prosecutions. But don't underestimate the difficulties in trying to break into an already saturated market. Issues for anyone intending to set up on their own account are:

◆ A robust (but cautious) business plan addressing the costs of setting up and running the new practice (including marketing) and where the income is expected to come from;

◆ If you are intending to go into business with someone else, you will need to enter into a written agreement with that person;

◆ Deciding whether to establish yourself as a sole-practitioner, partnership, LLP or limited company;

◆ Find out which prospective clients are actually going to instruct you;

◆ Tackling the hardest question about what you will do if it all goes wrong. Suppose the reception room remains empty and the telephones silent? Suppose that the only incoming email is the one advertising Viagra? How are you going to pay the bills?

Fortunately entrepreneurial lawyers now have a virtual-alternative to setting up their own firms in the form of a brand-new business-model. Under this model lawyers work as self-employed consultants with an established firm, which acts like a hub. The self-employed consultant will still be responsible for getting, doing and invoicing their own work. But the hub firm will deal with the central office administration including managing client money and obtaining professional insurance cover. It frees up the consultant lawyer from the administrative burden of running a legal practice, which means that they can get on with the business of earning money. In return the hub firm takes a cut of the consultant-lawyer's fee income, which can still leave that lawyer with up to 70% of fees earned. The hub-firm's own office overheads are also lower because each of the consultant-lawyers will be responsible for making their own working arrangements.

A third way is the locum market. Every year there are exhausted lawyers taking holidays. There are lawyers going on maternity leave. These are planned absences. But there are also lawyers falling off motor-bikes or breaking their legs in skiing accidents. All these absences need to be covered and service continuity maintained. For short term absences, a lawyer-colleague may pick up the reigns. For anything longer, someone may need to be recruited at short-notice to fill the gap. This is the essence of the locum market. It is about taking on someone who is already fully trained and who can take on an unfamiliar work-load and run with it. But it is not just about short term cover. Some organisations, particularly local authorities, make heavy use of locums to provide extra resource during peak-workloads, which can be most of the time. Those assignments are longer. For locum work it is 'easy in' and 'easy out'.

Most locums work through agencies. They are not employed by the end-user directly. They will either be employed through a contract with the agency or through an 'umbrella company', in which the locum pays the company a weekly fee for acting as their employer and making the required deductions of income tax and national insurance contributions. Until recently there were significant tax advantages for locums working through their own personal-service companies and obtaining their remuneration in the form of dividends instead of by way of a monthly pay cheque. But this tax advantage has since been neutralised by what has become known as IR35, where Revenue and Customs deem long-term self-employed locums to be employees of the organization for whom they are providing services.

Lawyers become locums for different reasons. It may provide a stop-gap for someone who is in between jobs. It offers flexibility for someone who only wants to work part of the year. It also provides income for older lawyers who may already be 'retired' from their permanent jobs but don't want their skills to become stale or evaporate. And why would you? Lawyering can be a job for life.

INDEX

Academic Stage 127.
Administrative Court 182.
Administration of Justice Act 1985 40, 141
Adversarial system 26, 27, 28, 29.
Advertising 157.
Agencies 157, 158.
Apprenticeship 99, 118, 119, 120, 121, 138.
Arnold v Britten 129.
Articled Clerk 15.
Associate 169.
Association of Personal Injury Lawyers 79.
Attorney 31, 32.
Authorised Practitioner 138, 139, 140.

Bar Course Aptitude Test 128, 129, 130.
Bar Professional Training Course 130, 131.
Barristers' Clerks 41, 42, 43, 44, 152, 153.
Bookshops 23, 24,25.

Bush House 19.

Called to the Bar 133.
Campbell v Gordon 130.
Celebrity lawyers 11, 12, 13, 14.
Chancery Lane 21.
Chartered Legal Executives 37, 38, 29, 40, 134, 135, 136, 137, 138, 139,140.
CILEX Practising Certificate 139.
CILEX route to qualification 121, 122, 123.
Clerks' Room 142.
Client Care letter 64, 65.
Common Professional Examination 105.
Company solicitors 57, 58, 80, 81, 165,161,165.
Compensation Fund 54
Communication 91, 92, 93, 94, 164, 165.
Conveyancing 66, 67, 68, 69.
Conveyancing Wars 9, 10.
Creative thinking 94, 95.

ABOUT THE AUTHOR

Charles Ward became a solicitor on 15th December 1976 and has worked in private practice, industry and local government. He currently works as a senior property lawyer with HB Public Law and is also Company Solicitor with the Institute of Cemetery and Crematorium Management. He has previously worked with Capsticks and Unilever Plc.

He began writing for publication in 1992 with a series of property-related articles for Legal Executive Journal; Estates Gazette and Local Government Chronicle. Between 1994 and 2000 he researched, wrote, and edited a weekly Law Page for Local Government Chronicle. He was also a Chief Examiner for the Chartered Institute of Legal Executives from 2006 to 2014, with responsibility for setting and overseeing the marking of the Level 3 Conveyancing Examination. He can be contacted at vivward@btinternet.com.

OTHER BOOKS
BY THIS AUTHOR

Local Authority Companies 1996

Published through LGC Communications (ISBN 0 904 677 77X) and at 92 pages, this was one of the first books written about local authority companies and the legal regime within which they operate.

Public Debt Management 1999

Published though LGC Communications (ISBN 0904677 885) and at 106 pages, the book's aim is to help public and other social creditors to develop and implement strategies to prevent and reduce arrears.

Residential Leaseholders' Handbook

Published in 2006 through EG Books (ISBN 0 7282 0490 8) and at 192 pages, this book explains in plain language everything leaseholders and their advisers need to know about long residential leases and leaseholder-rights.